Yanks

Over Europe

Yanks Over Europe

American Flyers
in World War II

Jerome Klinkowitz

THE UNIVERSITY PRESS OF KENTUCKY

Scholarly publisher for the Commonwealth,
serving Bellarmine College, Berea College, Centre
College of Kentucky, Eastern Kentucky University,
The Filson Club, Georgetown College, Kentucky
Historical Society, Kentucky State University,
Morehead State University, Murray State University,
Northern Kentucky University, Transylvania University,
University of Kentucky, University of Louisville,
and Western Kentucky University.

Editorial and Sales Offices: The University Press of Kentucky
663 South Limestone Street, Lexington, Kentucky 40508-4008

Library of Congress Cataloging-in-Publication Data

Klinkowitz, Jerome.
    Yanks over Europe : American flyers in World War II / Jerome
Klinkowitz.
        p.   cm.
    Includes bibliographical references and index.
    ISBN 0-8131-1961-8
    1. World War, 1939-1945—Aerial operations, American.
2. World War, 1939-1945—Aerial operations, British.
3. World War, 1939-1945—Campaigns—Europe.   4. World War,
1939-1945—Personal narratives, American.   I. Title.
D790.K565   1996
940.54'21'092—dc20   95-52483

To the memory of Aunt Donna,

a flyer's wife

Contents

Acknowledgments

Although *Yanks Over Europe* is a study of the written record, of how American flyers of the Eighth and Fifteenth Air Forces composed their memoirs of flying from England and the Mediterranean to fight the Axis powers in World War II, several veterans of this conflict have sent me letters, telephoned, visited with me, or welcomed me into their homes for talks about the air war. These have included Leroy Newby (a bombardier on B-24s), Alan F. Kelsey (an air gunner in the Royal Air Force on Wellingtons and Lancasters), Clyde B. East (a Mustang pilot), Dr. D.W. McLennan (a flight leader in the Royal Canadian Air Force), Don Charlwood (a navigator on Lancasters for the Royal Australian Air Force, serving in England with the RAF), and John Richards (a Coldstream Guardsman with a special interest in the air battles above his home in Plymouth). My interest in American narratives has grown from initial studies of RAF and Luftwaffe stories, and these gentlemen have helped me understand the transition.

Collecting the published documents studied here has been a complex task. Some were issued by major commercial houses, and a few were best-sellers. But many have appeared with small specialty publishers, and some of the most important have been independently published by the authors themselves. In other fields the suspect nature of "vanity publishing" quite properly deflects critical interest; for air combat memoirs just the opposite applies, for several good reasons. First of all, the authors in question are not frustrated professional writers; in almost all cases the work in question is the only book the author ever wishes to write. Secondly, such authors are well outside the professional stream of agents, editors, and other contacts so instrumental in placing a book. But most important is the fact that the typical memoirist feels very strongly about the personal nature of his story. He is telling it for truth, not for profit; for his own satisfaction, not for any sense of glory. Self-publishing is therefore a natural vehicle for such authors, who can retain full control of their material. This is why the self-published book may in the end be the most reliable, at least when it comes to reflecting personally on the air war.

Then too there is the half-century during which such writings have appeared. The first book treated here was published in 1941, two years before I was born. For tracking down both old, out-of-print volumes and the sometimes uncatalogued small press and self-published volumes, I am grateful to Julie Huffman-klinkowitz for her research skills and to these specialist book dealers: Brian Cocks of Helpston, Peterborough, in England's Cambridgeshire, and the Owens Book Centre of Tavistock, Devon; Crawford-Peters Aeronautica of San Diego, California; and Zenith Books in Osceola, Wisconsin.

Sole support for my scholarship has come from the University of Northern Iowa. I am grateful to the English Department, College of Humanities and Fine Arts, and especially to the Graduate College, which provided several research fellowships that allowed me to complete this work.

Introduction

Vets

THE PLANES ARE STILL with us, flying into regional airports across the United States every summer. Sometimes it's for an air show, where they take their place among the fragile biplanes of an earlier era and the supersonic fighters here for a dazzling display of military aerobatics. More often they are by themselves or in tandem with another ship, barnstorming their way from field to field on a money-raising tour that keeps them in flight.

War birds. Ghost squadrons. The sight is still spectacular, even when the B-17, the Flying Fortress once fancied as the mightiest plane aloft, taxies by the terminal ramp and proves no bigger than a modern thirty-seat commuter plane. And look how well a P-51 Mustang can perform, drawing oohs and aahs from the crowd as it overflies the runway at less than forty feet, then pulls back to rocket nearly straight up for a breathtaking 5,000-foot climb. There are no aircraft on the commercial ramp that can do that.

Then there are the vets, the old guys who've come out to see the planes they once flew. They're still with us, too. But only for a time. Once they were everywhere, their experiences so common that no one thought to talk about them. Now, fifty years after the last World War II missions were flown, their numbers have thinned considerably. But they are easier to spot now, and more frequent in their appearances, for they're retired, with time on their hands. What better way to spend it than coming out to the airport. Perhaps some of them have been out in the yard that morning, raking leaves or watering the bushes, when the sound of four Pratt and Whitney or Wright engines has made them think they're daydreaming back to Lavenham Aerodrome in England or Foggia Main in Italy where last they heard this distinctive roar. Others have read about it in the paper and planned the day for weeks. Either way, here they are, paying their seven dollars to come in and have a look. And what a look it is.

The B-17, painted olive drab, sits angled just past the fence. Beyond it, a silvery B-24 squats on its tricycle gear. A string of brightly colored pennants guides visitors to a stairway at the B-17's nose and another at the B-24's bomb bay, for those who want to hand over another three bucks and take the tour inside. That's where all the kids and parents head, eager for a glimpse of the real war. But the veterans aren't doing that, at least not yet. They have other places on their minds.

Five or six are standing at each plane's nose, talking knowledgeably about Sperry and Norden bombsights. An equal number cluster at the tail, patting its protruding gun barrels and telling stories about feed belts and electrically heated flight suits. Stepping back, one sees groups of men at each crew station. There is no question that here is where they served, where they flew upwards of twenty-five to fifty missions over Nazi Europe. Most are happy, jawing away about the various technologies the way they'd otherwise be comparing features on their RVs. This is what one hears, passing from group to group, rather than war stories the little kids think the inside of each plane holds. At most, one of the talkers might pause for a bit, then reflect on how he loved that Fortress or Liberator because it always got him home. But that's all.

A caution: if a solitary vet is seen, off by himself at the ball turret or waist gun, don't intrude. Chances are he's in tears.

As the day lengthens, a few stories emerge. A manufacturer's representative, one of the factory troubleshooters attached to each fighter or bomber group, looks up at the tail-gun position of the B-24 and recalls wryly how that's the way he flew home, in a war-weary Liberator all the way across the Atlantic. That, plus endless journeys on the hard bench seats of C-47s and in the steel buckets of C-54s, has made him so sick of aviation that his wife can't talk him into flying to Hawaii. Up front, two pilots exchange stories of notorious malingerers in their crews who always disappeared when it came time for the arduous work of pulling the props through several cycles before starting engines, clearing oil from the cylinders. What theme there is, is simple: that we survived. Just like these old planes here today. Indeed, the planes seem almost party to their conversations. Everyone is happy and no one wants to talk about those that went down.

Then, after the crowds have thinned, the gentlemen reach for their wallets and step up for a look inside. The young man, wearing the contemporary flight togs and sculpted sunglasses that suggest he's the one who flew this baby in today, waves off their dollars. Taking ladder steps where once they boosted themselves into the nose, the vets glimpse into the plexiglass enclosure that frames the navigator and bombardier positions, then climb on up to the second stage landing from where they can lean into the cockpit. Next they move back through the fuselage, passing the radio room after stepping nimbly down the catwalk that spans the bomb bay. At midship the waist gun positions are open to a light breeze, nothing like the 200 mile-per-hour (mph) gale of subzero winds endured aloft. There's a door to the tail-gun position, but it's closed. So turn left and exit through the crew door just a few steps above the ground.

Has everyone had a look? Not quite yet, for standing in the shadows of the top turret position is a small, fit-looking old man wearing a light jacket. A little boy has come up into the nose and, at eye level, spots the patch sewn on.

"Mister," he asks, "why do you have a bird on your jacket?"

The old vet quietly explains that this was the emblem of his fighter squadron—politely, but not eager to add much else.

"What kind of bird is it?" the boy asks.

"It's an eagle," the veteran answers. Then, seeing that he's sparked interest from another onlooker, realizes he owes posterity a few more words from history. "I was in what was called an Eagle squadron," he adds. "We flew airplanes called Spitfires."

"Neat-o!" the kid exclaims, then turns to busy himself with the guns.

Having spoken, however, the old gentleman has come out of himself, as it were, and finds it easier to chat with others. His comments are those of apology: he's been here on the turret deck long enough, he'll move on so others can see. But the rush is over, he's assured; the crowds have mostly left. So why not continue to spend some time here, as he confesses to have been doing.

He says a few more words about the Eagle squadrons and stops a moment to think about how rare such experiences were. Only 244 Americans got to fly in these three outfits as prewar volunteers to the Royal Air Force (RAF). Well past fifty years later, how many of them can still be left? If they're all as healthy looking as this man, probably quite a few.

But it's obvious the old Spitfire pilot's thoughts are elsewhere now. Still apologizing for the time he's taking here, he quietly explains what has made him linger.

"Later on, when the first American bombers came over," he says in the now eerily quiet fuselage, "our squadron escorted them on their first missions across the English Channel." Those would have been B-17 Flying Fortresses, just like the one he's standing in now. But for him today's experience is special.

"The bombers were based at different airfields," he notes. "We'd meet them after takeoff and follow them out, or else fly up to meet them as they began to return." He pauses for a moment. "We didn't have their range," he reflects.

They surely didn't. And because those B-17s had to continue on to heavily defended targets alone, many were cut to ribbons. Losses were so high that the daylight strategic bombing offensive was almost abandoned soon after it began.

But the Fortresses flew on, taking time to regroup and then mounting another dangerous mission. Spitfire escorts stayed with them as long as possible, doing the best they could. The suffering must have been enormous.

Is that why the gentleman is looking over this plane today?

"In all these years," he says softly, "I never saw one close, closer than from the air." Never even on the ground, for the bombers took off from bases in East Anglia, whereas the Eagle squadrons were at Duxford or elsewhere in Cambridgeshire or Essex.

And so this barnstorming tour of two ancient bombers has closed a circle for a quiet old gentleman, a person unique to this crowd and as rare a war bird as these aircraft here today.

"This is the first time I've been inside a B-17," he clarifies, then slips back into silence as he stares out the turret dome and past the wing, looking out to where he would have flown his Spitfire over fifty years before. Perhaps he's wondering how the top gunner felt when that Spitfire, its fuel reserves depleted, winged over and headed back to England.

His auditor moves on, leaving the man alone with his memories, reminding himself of stories that only in special instances will be told.

Stories from these veterans have been long in coming. This delay and the nature of these stories themselves have to do with what the air war was and how it was fought. Needless to say, there was no other war quite like it. Far more so than the First World War, this was a global conflict. Global in geography, and also global in demo-graphics: civilians were involved more than any time before or after, both as enlistees in military service and as contributors to the war effort. At least in the European Theater of Operations (ETO), a factory was as likely to be bombed as an airfield. And not just a factory making planes or tanks: anything that went into a piece of military equipment or made it go was a fair target, including manufacturers of ball bearings, steel, and electrical equipment, not to mention petroleum refineries. Likewise for the infrastructure of roads, railways, bridges, canals, and port facilities.

Even the air war was of ordinary people, on the ground and in the skies. In the United States Army Air Force (USAAF), created from the absolutely minimal prewar Army Air Corps (USAAC), professionals were outnumbered by tens of thousands to one. Officers were not even given reserve commissions, but temporary assignments in an expediency called the Army of the United States, meant to be dissolved after hostilities.

In today's Air Force of computerized supersonics, learning to fly a fighter proficiently takes as long as studying to be a doctor. In 1942 aviation cadets were soloing in six to ten hours, getting their initial training in contracted civilian flying schools. A few more months of basic and advanced training within the military taught them skills that they'd polish while preparing for shipment abroad. Often in less than a year, they'd be flying from bases in England or North Africa, tangling with careerists from the early Luftwaffe. It was not considered an unfair fight, and plenty of young Americans fresh from high school or taken out of their sophomore college years were shooting down veterans of the Condor Legion who'd been aces since the Spanish Civil War.

This could happen because the machinery was powerful but not overwhelmingly complex. There was nothing in a B-17 bomber except the bombsight that could not be manufactured, at least in principle, from what was available in a neighborhood hardware store. Its ten 500-pound bombs hardly added up to apocalyptic destruction, and the plane's 200 mph cruising speed was not beyond the mind's comprehension, especially when some of its pilots may have been hot-rodding in excess of 100 mph back home just a year before. Its instruments were understandable in theory to anyone who read *Popular Mechanics*. Pilots, navigators, bombardiers, and others in the crew were not rocket scientists; they were ordinary people, being asked to do something that took courage but was well within their limits of performance.

And there were so many of them. From the start of hostilities planners hoped that victory over the Axis powers was a matter of attrition. Production would be the key: of aircraft by the hundreds of thousands, and of trained personnel to match. It was an entirely different kind of war than fought the year before by the British, where the fabled few of RAF Fighter Command repulsed a tactically oriented, short-range, and lightly armed Luftwaffe. Aerial engagements from the Battle of Britain can be detailed in a few dozen pages, including names of adversaries and serial numbers of their planes. The battle itself lasted from mid-July to late October, with the bomber assault on London and other cities continuing until the following May. During this time, 25,000 Londoners perished—counting other targets in Britain, 40,000 in all. The responsive assault on Germany lasted three years. During this period any one target in the Reich, within any twenty-four hour period, received the total tonnage of bombs that Goering's Luftwaffe dropped on London during the entire ten-month Blitz. Given that this was a war of attrition, the Allies were determined not to lose. Nine hundred thousand Germans died in the raids that proved it.

As a result, Americans flying in this war were not "the few" who could be glamorized and individualized in the way Churchill had made his own pilots seem like Arthurian knights. This was democracy's war, and it was fought democratically. And as a result, not that many American veterans of the European air war felt compelled to tell their story, so widely had the experience been shared. When the press did focus on someone equivalent to the RAF's Johnnie Johnson or Douglas Bader, such as Don Blakeslee and Don Gentile, their notoriety did not survive the war—Gentile perishing in a flying accident, Blakeslee remaining silent. Although a few memoirs were published in the 1950s, there was nothing to equal the parade of best-sellers issued by the RAF illuminaries during this time. The one American ace who did garner postwar fame was Chuck Yeager, and that was because of his exploits as a rocket pilot breaking the sound barrier and pushing manned flight to the edge of space.

The memoirs that exist from the war years and the decades immediately afterwards are therefore documents to treasure. The first—published in 1941 and 1942 by Americans who, even before the Eagle squadrons, volunteered to fly and fight for the British in the RAF—are significant for their contrast with the stories of English pilots. Even though flying the same Hurricanes and Spitfires in some of the same squadrons, no American pilot responded in the manner of Richard Hillary's *The Last Enemy* (1942), Paul Richey's *Fighter Pilot*

(1941), and Brian Lane's *Spitfire!* (1942), even though these books were being read at home. Because they were being read, in fact, the first Americans "over here" may have felt compelled to establish the differences in their own narratives. And that they did, starting a tradition that continued with the subsequent stories told by the first Americans to have their own units in the RAF: the men of the three Eagle squadrons serving from October 1940 to September 1942.

A decade later, when British publishers were blessed with such classics as Johnnie Johnson's *Wing Leader* (1956) and Paul Brickhill's biography of Douglas Bader, *Reach for the Sky* (1954), American readers could find little of their own. Perhaps it was the anticlimactic nature of the Korean War, where objectives and heroics were so less well defined, that dampened the spirit. Not that the air war in Korea lacked possibilities for mythification, including the largely untold story of two unique figures in their Marine jets flying combat missions as a team: the already famous baseball player Ted Williams and future astronaut John Glenn. Instead, Americans took interest in the ongoing careers of two veterans—a bomber pilot from the Pacific and a Mustang ace of the ETO—because their efforts were inclined not backward to stories of the war but forward to crossing barriers of sound and space: William Bridgeman's *The Lonely Sky* (1955) and Chuck Yeager's collaboration with William R. Lundgren, *Across the High Frontier* (1955).

Chuck Yeager's story has stayed with us—dormant during the Vietnam War years of the sixties and early seventies, but emerging into regained splendor as part of Tom Wolfe's *The Right Stuff* (1979) and his self-titled *Yeager* (1985). Here, with decades of military uncertainty almost over and a cold war victory coming into sight, the story of an old Mustang ace from World War II becomes interesting in a uniquely current way. Wolfe's thesis is that ground-controlled spaceflight fought an emergent struggle with the legend of pilot-directed test flying, and Yeager himself establishes how that test-pilot tradition developed from the fighter exploits of World War II. Here, forty years after the events, a dynamic for telling such stories first became available to the veterans of America's air war of 1942-45. No longer were they common stuff, old stuff. Just the opposite: theirs has become the first chapter of what is America's most glorious post-war future.

Two other factors figure in. Fifty years after the last World War II combat mission, there are not many of these flyers left. There are enough to form talkative little klatches at each traveling B-17 exhibit, and plenty enough to tell marveling onlookers that yes indeed a

Mustang could zoom into the sky like that way back in 1944, but not so many that their experience can be shared widely. Once it could, but now the other great campaign of attrition, time's persistent war against us all, has made them quite a bit more rare. Perhaps, when they were youngsters in the 1920s, there were some Civil War veterans around, with no one especially interested in their stories. Then they became young men, and their own war intervened, and next time they looked those veterans of the Union and Confederate armies were gone. The Eagle squadron pilot picturing how his Spitfire looked from inside this battered bomber is today's equivalent of a figure from his own youth, a gray-haired veteran of General Meade's Army of the Potomac come back sixty years after Gettysburg to look down from a hillside on the field that was the site of Pickett's Charge.

Veterans of our own century's greatest war are also becoming scarce. But here is the second factor significant in their coming to speak now: the last few years have ushered in their retirements, allowing time for things like air shows and the type of reminiscence such shows inspire. In the leisure of its retirement this generation provides an audience for an entire category of cable television programming, one that reexamines World War II from every possible perspective. And younger generations watch along, fascinated by this glimpse of what happened within living memory.

It is from retirement, by a generation getting ready to take its leave of the American scene, that the greatest number of World War II stories are being told. And some very fascinating ones are told from the perspective of the air. Debates continue over the effectiveness of that air war, particularly in its strategies. But no one can deny that the air campaign constituted America's most visible presence. The common description of England during these years is that it became a gigantic aircraft carrier for the Allied assault on Nazi Germany. And what massive formations were sent off, groups of bombers whose basic unit numbered as three and then six dozen, stretching in a stream sometimes 100 miles long. Around them coursed hundreds of fighters, some of them (like the P-47 Thunderbolt) weighing as much as the Luftwaffe bombers that had blitzed London a few years before. The Normandy invasion's D-day assemblage is said to have provided a mammoth spectacle; but from late in 1943 onwards American air power sent vast armadas into German airspace almost every day, with the RAF there to continue the pounding at night.

Historiographers, those concerned with what part of a story is told (and how), may argue for a third factor in the renaissance of

World War II memoirs published in the past ten years. Earlier times may have privileged histories written by or about the leaders, the "great men" instrumental in the turn of events. In the years following the Civil War we had memoirs from General Grant and others of his stature. In 1949 "Hap" Arnold, General of the Air Force, published his own reminiscence, which in his case had the appropriate title of *Global Mission* (1949). Arnold's story is important, but for our age it need not stand alone. The global nature of this air war, as we have seen, depended on the contributions of not just professionals but also average people—*that* was why it was global.

Yesterday, the story was *Global Mission.* Today the story is that of *Fletcher's Gang, Zemke's Wolf Pack, Target Ploesti: View from a Bombsight,* and *A Wing and a Prayer.* This shift is reflected in the television documentaries as well: no longer do we have *The Big Picture* or the massive sweep of *Victory at Sea,* but rather *Fighter Pilot's Story,* a video self-produced by P-47 pilot Quentin Aanenson and broadcast by Public Broadcasting Service (PBS) stations in June 1994. Aanenson's story, like the book-length memoirs of the air war, covers just his part of the war. But today such limitations are seen as a benefit, for no preconceptions or overriding theses are allowed to deflect the realism of detail. Many an author begins by saying that during his time in service he had very little idea of what was happening at large. Even on their own missions, flyers lacked the full picture, for a squadron of Mustang fighters might break up in a dogfight and wind up ranging over hundreds of miles apart, while within a single bomber the navigator could be experiencing something entirely different from what the tail gunner saw.

None of these authors has a political point to make. Almost none of them, in fact, even have a specific strategy to argue or tactic to defend. Rather, their method is inductive. Far from the carefully arranged deductions of Hap Arnold in *Global Mission,* the writers of *Target Ploesti* and *Fletcher's Gang* must learn about the war as it happens. Their story is its own epistemology, its own coming to knowledge, which makes it specially appealing to the reader who may wish to learn something but doesn't relish being lectured to. Leroy Newby, Eugene Fletcher, and the other memoirists whose works are studied here must instead consider what they've seen and put parts together from what their friends have seen and said. Crew members of a B-17 or B-24 stretch out on their bunks or cycle into the village for a pint of beer, comparing notes on the mission they've just flown. Fighter pilots like Chuck Yeager and Bud Anderson park their Mustangs on the hardstand and do the same thing. Little by little a bigger picture emerges, but never at the cost of the small, sometimes anomalous details, details that today suggest what the war was really like.

Perhaps the authors felt such stories were unfashionable or methodologically incorrect during those first decades after the war. The different nature of the RAF's air combat—almost man-to-man during the Battle of Britain, then in the enforced isolation of strategic night bombing afterwards—did put focus on the individual.

Johnnie Johnson and Douglas Bader were great men. So were Guy Gibson and the Dam Busters, Don Bennett and the Pathfinder Force. And so their stories could be welcomed forty years ago in an especially celebrity-conscious age.

But today, when historians and documentary filmmakers dig through fragments of the past to find diaries not only by military leaders but also by common foot soldiers from the Civil War, veterans of World War II's air combat have found a readership for their stories. And what interesting stories they are.

Although filled with action and rich in military detail, these memoirs are wealthier still in their personal dimension. Sometimes the nature of these flyers' war strikes them as overwhelming, such as when a freshly trained crew member just landed in England sees a massive formation of B-17s pass overhead on its way to Germany. Other times the hype worked an opposite effect, such as when a fighter-bomber pilot, going into action near the end of the war, flies his first mission across the lines into Germany itself. Expecting to find a mighty fortress beneath his wings, he encounters something quite different: farm fields, tree-lined roads, and little villages just waking up in the gentle morning haze.

In each case the reader has learned something important about the war, something important but contradictory: that the enemy abroad is such a mighty threat that the world's greatest gathering of power must be massed and sent against it, but also that this enemy is not a firebreathing monster but someone whose home looks much like anyone else's.

There is a gap between such contrary realizations, a gap that flyers' stories fill today.

Chapter 1

Eagles

THERE WERE NOT MANY of them, these American pilots who were the first of their countrymen to fly combat missions from England during World War II—far less than even "the few" Winston Churchill memorialized as his country's saviors in the Battle of Britain, a battle that was just ending in October 1940 when the first of three volunteer Eagle squadrons became operational with the Royal Air Force. As microcosmic as the Battle of Britain was, consisting on the British side of scarcely 700 fighters flown by just over 1,000 pilots, the American numbers were even smaller: only 244 flyers (in the company of sixteen British pilots, most attached as initial commanders and flight leaders). The attrition rate, as one might expect, was horrendous; 108 did not survive the war. But fifty years later a rewarding statistic exists: of the 136 who did come home in 1945, some to continue in Air Force careers or high-risk flying jobs, more than eighty were still alive half a century later.

Stories told by veterans of the Eagle squadrons make an unusual but insightful first chapter in the narratology of the Second World War. Unlike the younger men brought into the Army Air Corps after Pearl Harbor, Eagle squadron volunteers were older, one (Harold Strickland) aged thirty-eight when recruited in 1940. Many had previous flying experience, a few were Army Air Corps rejects or washouts, and nearly all were vastly more experienced at life than the average twenty-year-old preparing to fly and fight after America entered the war. The sense of independence that brought them to

England sometimes rubbed roughly against RAF practice, and their own exclusion from Air Corps tradition made later integration into the USAAF's Fourth Fighter Group less than easy. For these reasons their stories are all the more remarkable.

Americans serving in the Royal Air Force attracted publicity even before the first Eagle squadron was formed. Seven U.S. citizens flew for the RAF in the Battle of Britain, and one—Arthur Gerald Donahue of rural St. Charles, Minnesota—published a book about it, *Tally-Ho! Yankee in a Spitfire* (1941). With an excerpt appearing in the *Saturday Evening Post* as early as 13 May 1941, Donahue's volume set the tone that distinguishes so many subsequent Eagle narratives. He himself was too adventuresome and independent to stay more than three weeks with the eventual Eagles, which reinforces the impression that Americans already enlisted in the RAF were so eager for action that a veteran such as Donahue could not wait for his newly arrived countrymen to be equipped. Instead he transferred back to an all-British squadron and soon shipped out for where the real action seemed to be: Singapore. Nevertheless, *Tally-Ho! Yankee in a Spitfire* defines what the essential Eagle narrative would be.

Like postmodern historiography itself, Art Donahue's story disclaims any sense of great-man heroism or monumentally important action. His first chapter is titled "A Farm Boy Goes Abroad" and begins with a warning that what follows is anything but blood-curdling or epic. What does follow are issues, themes, and structures that characterize the American experience flying with the RAF against the Luftwaffe over England and the Channel. A commercial flyer since age eighteen and a private flight instructor with air time on his country's latest style of planes, Donahue was nevertheless frustrated in his attempts to join the USAAC Reserve. And so at the time of Dunkirk and the fall of France, in June 1940, he crossed into Canada for what was advertised as a "noncombatant job" (p. 4) with the Royal Air Force. In England, his signature made him a commissioned officer, and a short advanced training course gave him qualification as a fighter pilot. By August 4 Donahue had arrived at No. 64 Squadron at Kenley, an active station south of London halfway to the coast from where some of the heaviest Battle of Britain engagements were joined. On August 5 Donahue met the enemy, his Spitfire taking a 20-mm cannon shell and being forced to land at the squadron's satellite base, Hawkinge. On August 12 Donahue was less fortunate, as his Spitfire was shot down and he bailed out with burns and other injuries. It was during his recovery that much of *Tally-Ho!* was written.

Given that a week in action was no mean attrition rate for Battle of Britain pilots, Donahue's experience is not unheroic in its scope. Yet combat itself is only part of any fighter pilot's story, and *Tally-Ho!* sets a proportion that tests out as almost perfectly right. Little is made of the fact that Donahue was spending June 1940 on a tractor cultivating corn, back on his father's farm as a break from flight instructing in Texas, only to find himself scarcely seven weeks later mixing with Messerschmitts over the English Channel. To move from a John Deere tractor to a Spitfire Mark I, the best performance fighter aircraft in the world at that time, is remarkable. Although Donahue was a qualified commercial pilot, that only makes it slightly less remarkable than a taxi or bus driver at Easter being given a short course, then being put behind the wheels of a race car at the Indianapolis 500 on Memorial Day. Consider that his Luftwaffe adversaries were regular officers in the world's strongest air force, most likely with combat experience already accrued in Spain, Poland, Norway, and the Battle of France. Little wonder that one of his first challenges faced in London was to learn how to salute, a task managed on the way back from a tailor's shop with the help of a friendly Women's Auxiliary Air Force (WAAF) treated to a Coca-Cola for her effort.

Of course Art Donahue doesn't know how to salute: it is a rubric of his times that few Americans serve in the tiny, peacetime army, with room for even fewer in the expensive business of flying pursuit aircraft. But here he is in England, fighting in the greatest air battle yet to happen in military history. As Col. James Saxon Childers noted just a few years later in *War Eagles* (1943), his contemporaneous account of the first Americans to arrive in more organized fashion, the British were suddenly introduced to what a nonprofessional, essentially citizen air force would be like:

> Despite their being in uniform, when the Eagles first arrived in England they were unmistakably civilians: military courtesy or discipline had almost no meaning at all for them. Old soldiers around the station were amazed at the behavior of these young Americans who, in some cases, were plain saboteurs of military tradition. They forgot to salute. They forgot to rise when a senior officer came into the room. They forgot to stand at attention when reporting to the C.O. And as for polishing their buttons—to hell with it (pp. 328-29).

Even more offensive than their lax military courtesy, the first American pilots radically disrupted the language of RAF valor. Although there were enough sergeant pilots from the Volunteer Reserve flying in the Battle of Britain to make it a somewhat leveling affair, popular imagery restricted the role and its ambiance to that of the upper classes: the professional, Cranwell-trained officers (for whom right school and family were essentials) and privileged, sometimes aristocratic members of the RAF Auxiliary squadrons, called (with admiration) gentlemen's flying clubs. Their language was that of actor David Niven, himself serving with the RAF but also starring as a Spitfire pilot with Leslie Howard in *The First of the Few*, a 1942 film that helped establish the legend of designer R.J. Mitchell's magnificent planes and the men who flew them.

Into this rarified atmosphere where combat had been characterized in the language of public school game days and lawn tennis matches came the Eagles, and Donahue before them, with an entirely different style of expression. Throughout *Tally-Ho!* he revels in images from the American mythos, feeling his plane "speeding up like a high-spirited horse that has been spurred" (1941, p. 53), seeing his squadron wheel toward the enemy "like a bunch of wild Indians" (p. 38), roaring away after a quick takeoff "like a stampeding herd of buffalo" (p. 55), watching an attacking Messerschmitt 109 "puffing blue smoke for all the world like a John Deere tractor!" (p. 57), and entertaining his squadron mates in the mess with renditions of "Carry Me Back to Old Virginny" (p. 155). Two years later, as a seasoned RAF veteran describing his further adventures in *Last Flight from Singapore* (1943), Donahue remains the quintessential American, he and his wingman fleeing a pack of Messerschmitts "like a couple of kids who'd just stolen a watermelon!" (p. 3), describing his squadron's Spitfires standing in their dispersal bays "like tired cavalry horses asleep" (p. 10), and himself and his colleagues as bursting into action like "a score of two-year-old colts from a Montana range . . . during the fresh new days of spring" (p. 13).

Almost every subsequent Eagle memoirist would write this way. One of the most outspoken, William R. Dunn, shows why in his own book, *Fighter Pilot* (1982). In the process of establishing an equivalent rank for his transfer from the Royal Air Force to the U.S. Army Air Force, he finds himself dealing with an old major general holding down a desk at the War Department, a man who turns out to be none other than the son of a famous Indian fighter who served in the same campaigns as Custer. As can be expected, the general speaks to young Mr. Dunn in the language of his father, warning the pilot that "You're going to run into a lot of Air Corps types who will be jealous of your RAF service and combat experience, and they'll try to shoot you out of the saddle, mark my words" (p. 112). As for praise, it's phrased as "In the old days you'd have made a good cavalryman, but now, these days, I can see the spirit is still there with you airmen. Good luck to you and good hunting. Keep a deep seat in your saddle and a tight rein" (p. 113). No wonder that Dunn and the other Eagles, plus Donahue before them, would use so many Wild West images in their writing. Churchill could compare his own RAF pilots to Arthurian knights, but had to reach back over a millennium for the reference. When Bill Dunn shakes hands with General Guy V. Henry, he is touching the frontier tradition, not just metaphorically but physically.

As far as the basics of wartime flying, however, Donahue's early narrative is directly on the mark. All that was already familiar in RAF narratives appears in *Tally-Ho!*: the danger of flying tail-end Charlie, the way blown-off gun patches told groundcrews their pilot had met the enemy, how battered Spitflies and Hurricanes would limp back to other RAF stations while those at home fields worried for their fates, how just seconds after the busiest dogfight the sky could become eerily clear of aircraft. There was the average day of wake-up, breakfast in the mess, assignment of flying duties, readiness at the flight's dispersal site (a hut out near the runways), the call for a scramble, takeoff, climb, switching on gunsight, the occasional engagement but more often tedium of eventless patrol, return, descent, and lunch before readiness again. There are especially prescient moments, such as when Donahue and some other pilots ride out to a farm "where a Messerschmitt had dived in the day before." All to be seen is a hole, with a few wing fragments in sight; the fuselage is farther down, and the engine farther still—"down about thirty feet!" Because the pilot had bailed out, Donahue speculates that "they probably wouldn't bother to dig it up" (1941, p. 82). Four decades later aviation enthusiasts would invent a new style of archaeology by doing just so.

Even more affecting is to read the author's comments on an otherwise nondescript sergeant pilot identified only as "Mann" (p. 60) who's hit with a cannon shell and worries about it because he has been flying the squadron leader's regular plane. Later on this same squadron mate is wounded in the hip and struggles back in an aircraft much more badly damaged (p. 96). Before the end of his story Donahue reports that "Sergeant Mann is not expected to be able to fly again. He was awarded the Distinguished Flying Medal while in the hospital" (p. 181). Almost half a century later, after indeed flying again as a career airline pilot and retiring to Beruit, Sergeant Pilot Jackie Mann was held by terrorists as a hostage, eventually released, and returned to England where he was honored with a Spitfire flypast.

Yet Donahue's status as an American gives him a unique perspective, one that helps him visualize the relativity of his circumstance in especially meaningful terms. As he relaxes in the warm August sun, lying in the grass near his Spitfire, Donahue assumes the familiar image of a Battle of Britain pilot from countless newsmagazine photographs of the time. That young men such as himself could in a few minutes time be called from such pastoral quiet to fight with German adversaries above is underscored by his habit of spending these idle moments picking shrapnel from his flying boots. But for him there is an even greater sense of contrast, for as he jots down these thoughts he looks at the notebook in his hands and has to force himself "to realize that I had bought it only three months before, in a drugstore in Manitowoc, Wisconsin" (p. 47). At this moment his best friend in the squadron asks for the notebook, where he writes down a girlfriend's name and phone number for notification should he die; needless to say, it is at this point in the narrative that Donahue anticipates sadly the time he will have to make just such a call.

Throughout both *Tally-Ho!* and *Last Flight From Singapore* Donahue exploits such perspective. An obvious marketing device, such references would appeal to American readers and make an otherwise unimaginable war more comprehensible to them. Thus in his second book the author makes much of flying his Hurricane in searing tropical heat while thirsting for "an ice-cold Coke or Orange Crush!" (1943, p. 28) and calculating how different the present January weather must be on his parents' Minnesota farm. As for the farm itself, Donahue does manage to revisit it even as he writes *Tally-Ho!*, as the RAF finds it politically advantageous to send him home for a brief spell early in 1941 to publicize Britain's war effort and appreciation of U.S. help. It was during this trip that Donahue visited magazine offices, gave interviews, and posed for pictures such as appeared in the *Saturday Evening Post* with the first excerpt from his narrative in progress. But, writer that he is, he cannot pass up opportunities to use perspective once again, this time from the opposite side as he notes during the visit with his folks:

> I did manage to spend a little time working on my father's farm, and it was strange to be doing the familiar tasks I knew so well on the farm just as if nothing had ever happened, while in my pocketbook I carried a little piece of pasteboard that read:

Return Ticket
Southern Railway
LONDON
(Charing Cross)
to
F—— (1941, p. 178).

That Donahue was shot down, suffered serious burns, and spent hospital time recovering provides another chance for him to view things from another side. Because he recuperates near Canterbury during the busiest weeks of the Battle of Britain, he hears and sometimes sees the aerial engagements that marked the Luftwaffe's most powerful onslaught and the RAF's heroically spirited defense. Lying abed during nighttime raids, his dreams become interactive when he reacts physically to an imagined Messerschmitt on his tail. Visual reactions are just as striking; he must struggle to realize "that at the head of each silver line curving across the sky five or six miles overhead is a pal who was sitting beside you in the pilots' hut a half-hour before," just as after his own sorties he has found it hard to identify with his own still-lingering smoke track "inscribed up there in the sky" (p. 99). When he returns to operations, it is with a similarly revised perspective, looking down from his cockpit and finding it "strange trying to realize that each of those weird moth-shaped, beautifully camouflaged creatures plummeting along and spurning back its vapor trail below me in this eerie frigid stratosphere was piloted by a pal of mine" (p. 130).

The highest compliment Art Donahue's imagination deserves is to note how it can put its author in the place of another: not just a fellow pilot in the squadron or even the RAF but as an enemy flyer with the Luftwaffe. When early in 1941 his unit begins their initial offensive sweeps across the Channel and into occupied France, Donahue pictures the confusion below as German pilots for the first time experience the type of raid English bases had suffered on a twice-daily basis less than half a year before. Granted, it makes him feel good that they were "getting some of their own at last" (p. 165), but his emphasis remains on the details of frenzied scurrying for equipment and hurried takeoffs that characterize the human drama this veteran knows so well. Perhaps it is motivated by familiar tales of chivalry and human decency that distinguish many early RAF narratives and which become far less frequent in Eagle squadron and especially later Eighth and Ninth Air Force accounts. From a December 1940 engagement Donahue has remarked how a captured German had to be stopped from destroying his Iron Cross, fearful as he was that the British would execute anyone so decorated; when told that merit was honored on both sides, the flyer insisted that his medal be sent to the Spitfire pilot who shot him down. But ultimately it is Donahue's ability as a writer that takes him where lesser talents might hesitate to go, including into the minds of his enemies.

Tally-Ho! includes great air combat scenes, but vivid description is also used for calmer matters. Taking off from coastal Hawkinge at dawn, Donahue is delighted to note the blue flames of his Spitfire's exhaust standing out against the dim countryside below, then to hover apparently motionless as the other planes drift into position around him as his flight forms up. "The sun, just rising and very red and big and beautiful, made weird lights over the tops of our camouflaged wings," he notes, adding that with the carpet of earth passing below "We were like a herd of giant beasts in some strange new kind of world" (p. 54). When a German raid comes in its noise is not of machinery but more like that of "a distant storm approaching—just a heavy, distant murmuring and rumbling that gradually grew louder" (p. 77) until eventually individual sounds could be discerned, including the high whine of escorting fighters. From the isolation of his hospital bed Donahue is able to trace the raid's progress by further aural cues: the bark of antiaircraft weapons, the staccato chop of Spitfire and Hurricane machine guns, and the answering bang from Messerschmitt cannons. Although his own combat descriptions have been vivid, the author does even better when listening in the dark, where for himself as well as for his reader he must compose what is taking place, including an interception high above:

> I would be listening to the humming of a Daimler-Benz cruising, and the *rhoom-rhoom* of a Rolls Royce turning pretty fast: and all at once there would be the roar of guns from a Spitfire or Hurricane. That would be answered instantly by the quick crescendo of the Daimler-Benz changing from its normal cruising right up the scale to its most agonized whine, over the space of about a second, as the surprised Nazi pilot "pushed everything forward" and opened up with every ounce of his engine's power to get away. The response was similar to that you get from stepping on the tail of a cat (pp. 78-79).

A similar passage comes eight pages later when after his release from hospital Donahue spends two nights in London—and experiences the urban terrors of the Blitz. It is with great relief that he moves on to some quieter recuperation time in the far southwest of Devon and Cornwall.

As promised in the first words of *Tally-Ho!*, Art Donahue's combat descriptions are anything but flamboyant. Although he dutifully records the details of his near-fatal encounter with the Messerschmitt that shot him down, including the disintegration of his Spitfire's instrument panel and the flash of a bullet sailing past his leg into the gas tank, he is most of all impressed by the "finality" of this salvo and the "silence" that ensues (p. 72). No matter that he has here and elsewhere mistaken his adversary for a Heinkel 113, a fighter that except for one widely photographed prototype existed only in faulty intelligence reports; such errors persist in occasional memoirs written as late as the 1990s. It is always the telling little detail rather than the overwhelming force of action that intrigues him: how RAF and Luftwaffe fighters "investigate each other" like strange dogs, "very much alert against hostile moves, circling sideways around each other until they decide whether or not they're going to be friends" (p. 113), and how in the thin air of high altitude the pilot loses power and the fine touch of control to the point of feeling "terribly unsubstantial," insecure, and in danger of "falling off into the eerie, seemingly limitless space below" (p. 125). Above all, Donahue can never forget that he is an American abroad, a civilian from a peacetime nation thrust so suddenly into what seems the century's most decisive battle to date. Even then, he declines to view it egotistically; instead, he'll spend an odd hour of leave time viewing the latest Hollywood film in London and feel like he's back home, only to step back out onto a blitzed-out street and realize that this, and not rural Minnesota, is the moment's reality.

As for Art Donahue's experience with the Eagles, it takes just two quick sentences in *Tally-Ho!* to recount; even at that, his brief experience with the formation of No. 71 Eagle Squadron, the first to be composed of American volunteers, is dismissed as "an outside factor" that "unfortunately interfered" with his plans to get back into action with his regular outfit, No. 64 Squadron (p. 97). His reluctance to say more speaks for his own humility and discretion; privately, he told another American pilot also going his own way that the Eagles seemed like "a motley crew that would never amount to anything," as reported by Vern Haugland in *The Eagle Squadrons: Yanks in the RAF, 1940-1942* (1979, p. 120). A more pressing matter was this initial Eagle squadron's delay in being equipped; with no Spitfires or Hurricanes in sight and the best hopes being only for some obsolete Brewster Buffaloes, Donahue transferred back to a conventional RAF unit as quickly as he could. Once there, he became bored with the new, post-battle phase of the war, and in order to avoid the tedium of dull convoy patrols opted for duty in the more active Middle East. This he got and more, making it all the way to Singapore in time to rally for its last, futile defense. His book about this part of his RAF service was begun during his long journey back to England, where he was posted to another squadron and eventually shot down and lost over the Channel on 11 September 1942.

Although *Tally-Ho!* tells the story of an American who was only briefly with the Eagles, it is nevertheless an accurate portrayal of the world in which such later memoirists as William R. Dunn, Richard L. "Dixie" Alexander, and James A. Goodson would find themselves. Immensely more problematic is the book long accepted as the first Eagle narrative, Byron Kennerly's *The Eagles Roar!* (1942). As a twenty-six-year-old roustabout with minimal flying experience, Kennerly resembled some of the more colorful types recruited by the Sweeny family as volunteers for the French Armée de l'Air and, after France fell in June 1940, as flyers for Great Britain. Such enlistments played havoc with neutrality rules and led to numerous complexities regarding citizenship, loyalty oaths, and other issues of national responsibility. But given American sympathy for England, volunteers for the Sweeny program made Atlantic crossings from Canada in sufficient numbers to form a squadron that was, except for its first commanding officer and flight leaders, all-American. This was the No. 71 Eagle Squadron that the veteran Art Donahue transferred out of on 23 October 1940, when equipment had been stalled and seemed long in coming; Kennerly joined it on 7 November, the day their Hurricanes finally arrived. From this position Kennerly wrote a stirring account of his and other Eagles' exploits. Indeed, it reads much like the bloodcurdling, shoot-'em-up epic Art Donahue disavows. What's problematic is that, according to the best available records, Byron Kennerly left the squadron before its first engagement. Only the real Eagles' distaste for self-glamorization of any kind kept the author's former squadron mates from commenting on the questionable nature of his book.

Kennerly's reputation as the just-emerging squadron's troublemaker is documented by Vern Haugland in his second volume about groups of American flyers serving in RAF units, *The Eagles' War: The Saga of the Eagle Squadron Pilots, 1940-1945* (1982). But to an American readership eager to show its post–Pearl Harbor patriotism, *The Eagles Roar!* was just the type of narrative needed in those difficult months of setback after setback in the Pacific. Even though England itself was in worse shape as submarine activity threatened to choke the island nation, the Battle of Britain could be mythologized as a rousing success. With its controversial bombing role yet to be undertaken, the Royal Air Force was at its most glamorous. Even more appealing was that a few Americans had beat their own country to the gun and were already flying and fighting over there. Having one of those flyers ready to crow about it made the book a marketer's dream. The Warner Brothers studio bought movie rights to Kennerly's story and produced it as *International Squadron* for release in October 1941, as the printed version was taking shape for the equally prestigious firm of Harper & Brothers. In the film, Byron Kennerly's role was played by no less a heroic star than Ronald Reagan; in his own narrative, Kennerly himself is equally imposing. That much of it's a lie seems to matter not at all, given the romanticized, unrealistic nature of most war movies rushed out at this time.

Read in the company of Art Donahue's more reliable narrative, *The Eagles Roar!* teaches a lesson about transposing fact into image more conclusive than any dismantling of popular cinema. Ronald Reagan never was an Eagle; Byron Kennerly was, at least for the recruitment, travel, and training phases, which for the Eagle experience remain the most crucial. Bogus as his combat scenes are, the author was in England for virtually everything else as No. 71 Eagle Squadron prepared to fight. Sent home in presumed disgrace as an incorrigible antidisciplinarian, he managed to transform himself into a hero simply on the basis of having been over to the hallowed ground of RAF achievement. His book's success is ironic proof that validity of combat description is not the key to understanding the essence of the Eagle squadrons' stories, legendary and realistic alike.

Myth-building starts with the volume's introduction, a historically styled summary written by "Charles Sweeny, Late Group Captain, Royal Air Force." This person is the flamboyant Colonel Sweeny who lied about his age to fight in the Spanish-American War, flunked out of West Point in 1899, served with the French Foreign Legion in 1914-15, rejoined the U.S. Army when America entered the Great War, and left the service as a lieutenant colonel. In 1939 he had in fact begun recruiting American volunteers to fly in the expected Battle of France and with the Finnish Air Force in the defense of that country. It was to one of Colonel Sweeny's covert invitations that Byron Kennerly first responded, a spooky business of vague notices posted at commercial airfields leading to discreet interviews in hotel suites around the country. When France fell, all this ended, to be resumed in immensely more effective fashion by the colonel's nephew, also named Charles Sweeny, who was presently living in London. The glamour of the younger Sweeny's life also taxes the powers of enumeration: wealthy expatriate businessman, brother and close social pal of golf champion Bobby Sweeny (who was at the time dating heiress and countess Barbara Hutton), and husband of a woman lyricized in Cole Porter's latest hit song. But for all this he was, unlike his uncle, a self-effacing sort, to the extent that thirty years would pass before his own role in organizing the first Eagle squadron was widely known. Instead, the uncle stepped forward to take credit, beginning with his introduction to Kennerly's book.

"The Eagle Flying Corps," as Colonel Sweeny incorrectly calls what was by now three regular RAF squadrons, "is the grandson in direct line of the Escadrille Lafayette of glorious memory" (p. vii). From this beginning (which fostered the misbelief, never corrected, that the colonel had flown with those heroes), Sweeny continues with his own history of negotiating with the French prime minister to command a similar *division etrangère*, the purpose of which would be to shake France out of her "phony war" lethargy and get to business in taking on the Germans before the Luftwaffe mounted an attack. Although Colonel Sweeny would have no part in the action, several flyers he recruited did make it to France, three of whom escaped the French debacle to fly with genuine glory as RAF pilots in the Battle of Britain: Vernon "Shorty" Keough, Andrew Mamedoff, and Eugene "Red" Tobin, whose names figure prominently in subsequent Eagle history (all perishing well before the Eagles transferred into the fledgling Fourth Fighter Group of the USAAF). But for Colonel Sweeny, sending more Americans over would be less for actual firepower than to "buck up English morale" (p. ix) and "awaken American people to the danger" (p. x) that a beleaguered Britain might otherwise accept peace on Hitler's terms. For Kennerly's volume he is able to list the first squadron's roster; although fudging the fact that it had a British and not American commander by describing squadron leader Walter Churchill as an "instructor" (p. xii), the old colonel (an American Colonel Blimp if there ever was one) levels with his readers about Art Donahue: "Within a few days he was transferred to his old Squadron at his own request. I hated to see him go. He is a mean little guy, with more poetry than meanness in his make-up. I saw in him the makings of an excellent Squadron Leader. I tried to stop his transfer, kicked like a base steer, but it did me no good" (pp. xii-xiii).

If indeed the Eagles looked to Donahue like "a motley crew that would never amount to anything," as Haugland reports, that impression may well have come from the likes of Byron Kennerly. Although undeniably the worst of the lot, he was not completely atypical; in fairness to him and the others, it must be emphasized that Art Donahue wrote as one of the very few avant-garde of American flyers in England. Blooded within the RAF in the exclusive company of British pilots and squadron personnel, he had a genuine part in the rare Battle of Britain experience. The Eagles came in groups of twenty or thirty at a time, enthusiastic for defending England but bringing their Americanisms intact and reinforceable. Hindsight offers the further advantage of seeing that however rowdy some of the Eagles were, their successors in the Eighth Air Force were perceived as much worse; from their behavior and not of the Eagles grew the judgment that these flyers were "overpaid, overfed, oversexed—and over here," all because each successive wave could not be romanticized so effectively as the last.

It is Kennerly's brashness that lets his style of storytelling get out of control. Housed in transit at what he chooses to call "one of the most luxurious of Canada's hotels" (p. 6), he spends his time partying on an unlimited expense account provided by the British government and limousine-hopping with celebrities. In England, the novelty of a camouflaged airfield with combat-ready Hurricanes dispersed beneath the trees strikes him as "quite a sight, airplanes in this Robin Hood setting" (p. 42). Taking the controls of one inspires not the thoughtful, delicate lyricism characteristic of other memoirists but rather the impression that "flying this aircraft was the nearest thing to riding a rocket I could imagine" (p. 103). When given the chance to meet and talk with a captured Messerschmitt pilot, Kennerly transcribes a conversation not from life but cobbled together from newsreel images and popular hysteria, including references to the "Heinkel 113, a new Nazi fighter, smaller than any other pursuit plane, but heavily gunned and very fast" (p. 39) that beyond its single-prototype existence never flew at all except in the fantasies of overimpressionable journalists. The RAF figures Kennerly encounters are all icons, including such faces from the picture post as Douglas Bader, Hugh "Cocky" Dundas, and (most improbably) Victoria Cross winner J.B. Nicolson. And although records show that Kennerly flew no operational missions at all, the ones he invents for himself are those American readers would know about, including not just the aerial defense of Coventry but a personal visit to the bombed-out city on the morning after. In the face of such references as a high-altitude engagement being called a "scramble" (p. 101) and a Hurricane's air-speed indicator a "speedometer" (p. 123), sharp-eyed readers should have suspected Kennerly's subterfuge. But in the early months of 1942 Americans were eager for news of any heroism whatsoever, and so such hocuspocus as memorial wreaths dropped from Hurricanes over the sea and Kennerly's own curious victory roll as "a final salute to the first casualty of the Eagle Squadron" (p. 204) could be accepted as fact.

Yet a certain amount of ill-discipline lets Kennerly make what can be read today as especially choice observations. From Bill Dunn's and other accounts, it has become apparent that at least one of the original Eagles emulated a different style of behavior. At the time Gregory A. "Gus" Daymond was much the media darling, the first Eagle to be fêted at home and a perennial favorite photographed with such visiting notables as Eleanor Roosevelt and King George VI. Mannered like a British aristocrat, Daymond had just the right image squadron intelligence officer J. Roland "Robbie" Robinson, a titled nobleman and Member of Parliament, wanted for the Americans he was shepherding through the realms of English influence. As a result, the rougher-edged Bill Dunn's indisputable claims as the first Eagle to down an enemy and then as the first Eagle ace were pushed aside so that the more presentable Daymond could win the requisite medals. When Vern Haugland sought an answer when preparing *The Eagle Squadrons* for publication in 1979, Daymond declined comment, telling the old and trusted war correspondent that he had "sold my life story to Warner Brothers in 1946, and they own the rights to my wartime experiences in toto" (p. 70). For Brig. Gen. Philip D. Caine's U.S. Air Force Academy history, *Eagles of the RAF: The World War II Eagle Squadrons* (1991), Daymond complied with a questionnaire but did not agree to an interview. Thus his side of things remains essentially untold. But what Bill Dunn's *Fighter Pilot* describes as a rather effetish clique among the more glamorous Eagles becomes in Byron Kennerly's book the behavior of an Eagle scout being pranked by one of the less self-taken boys:

> One pilot had a little "trouble" of a different kind during his first weeks at the station. It was Gus Daymond, the nineteen-year-old youngster of the squadron. He looked his age and this worried him. Doggedly he kept shaving with a safety razor, hoping each day he might harvest at least a trace of a crop. One day I removed the blade from his razor. For a week he continued his bladeless shaving, finally discovering what had happened.

Whenever he appeared, the fellows would start feeling their chins and sadly shake their heads. For several days he refused to speak to me (1942, p. 132).

Therefore *The Eagles Roar!* does have merit in terms of contributing to the overall picture of American squadron life. As far as its Hollywood fodder, neither the book or the film were worth the real Eagles' time. When an officially sanctioned but scarcely less romantic movie titled *Eagle Squadron* (1942) and starring Robert Stack was released, not even the director's use of their own flying sequences and cine-gun footage could make the results palatable to the flyers' tastes. At the London premier most of them walked out and resolved to stop talking to the press, with the result that news of the American Eagles took second place to more readily available accounts from the American Volunteer Group making waves as the Flying Tigers in China.

It is only in the 1980s that the more accurate Eagle narratives emerge. Significantly, just one is by an acknowledged celebrity, Eagle veteran and Fourth Fighter Group ace James A. Goodson. His *Tumult in the Clouds* (1983) has much about the later war, though it does include accounts of seeking combat before Pearl Harbor and of serving with the third and last Eagle squadron, No. 133. More indicative of a new attitude toward history are William R. Dunn's 1982 memoir, *Fighter Pilot*, and Richard L. Alexander's *They Called Me Dixie* (1988), for neither Dunn or Alexander had begun their service careers as officers and both felt that fact was held against them, keeping them out of the limelight reserved for media-styled heroes such as Goodson. Combined with Art Donahue's and Byron Kennerly's stories and in the company of three generations of Eagle histories (published by James Saxon Childers during the war, Vern Haugland in 1979 and 1982, and Philip D. Caine a full half century after the events themselves), these narratives by Goodson, Dunn, and Alexander cover the Eagles almost from top to bottom. Where they diverge is understandable; where they reinforce each other is rewarding; but when from positions of great divergence these memoirs intersect today's reader shares the magical effect of almost being there as witness.

Each came to the Eagle squadrons differently. Jim Goodson's decision to fly and fight was the most dramatic. With close ties to the United Kingdom, he'd been traveling abroad during the summer of 1939 and was sailing home on the ship *Athenia* when Prime Minister Neville Chamberlain's declaration of war was broadcast; Goodson begins his memoir with an account of hearing it in the ship's third class lounge and being told by a fellow passenger that "we're well out of it" (1983, p. 13). This sentiment remains widely shared even as the American and Canadian passengers catch a last glimpse of the Outer Hebrides, listen to a young Scotsman sing appropriate songs, and admit to a "great sense of nostalgia for old places and beloved faces" (p. 14). Within hours, however, the *Athenia* is torpedoed and Goodman finds himself in the thick of World War II, fighting for his own life but in even greater distress at the calamity visited on this unarmed, fully civilian liner:

> For the first time, I felt an overwhelming fury that was to sweep over me time and time again during the war. No one had the right to cause such suffering to innocent people. At first my rage was against the Germans, but later, when I saw the same suffering among their innocents, my fury was against those who used their power with such callous lack of responsibility to heap personal tragedy on the little people who wanted only to live. . . . No one had the right to cause such suffering, and those who assumed that right had to be stopped and punished. That was the vow; simple and profound; corny and devout (p. 25).

The paradoxes Goodson mentions are the key to his book's title, for a "tumult in the clouds" is the "lonely impulse of delight" that has drawn him, like William Butler Yeats' Irish airman of the First World War, to serve unbidden by claims of nationality or law.

Bill Dunn's were more professional: as the nephew of a World War I flyer, he grew up with military aviation as his goal. Twice he enlisted with such hopes, first in the U.S. Army (where he was stuck in the peacetime infantry from 1934 to 1937) and then beginning in September 1939, with the Seaforth Highlanders of the First Canadian Division, at the time the only way for an American citizen to get into the fray. Although the Royal Canadian Air Force (RCAF) would soon after accept American enlistments, Dunn earned his wings the hard way, crossing the Atlantic with a mortar unit for service in the Battle of France at Brest, from where he was evacuated to a holding camp near Borden in Hampshire. Here, on 16 August 1940, the Luftwaffe attacked; after dive bombers killed an antiaircraft crew, Dunn took over their Lewis gun and shot down two Stukas. Thus his first face-to-face encounter with his adversaries reads much like a Battle of Britain narrative, even though he's been tethered to the ground:

> The two Germans in the last Stuka survived the crash-landing and were captured. Next day I took a couple packs of cigarettes to them when I paid them a visit at the hospital. The pilot, a

young Feldwebel (Flight Sergeant) named Clausen, had his hands burned a bit. The air gunner—I've forgotten his name—had been wounded in the leg by a .303 round. Clausen spoke pretty good English, and he didn't seem too sore at me for shooting him down. The other guy, a typical Squarehead bastard, wouldn't even thank me for the cigarettes. We two, Clausen and I, talked about flying for a while. He said he tried to become a fighter pilot, but got stuck in dive bombers. I told him that I wanted to be a pilot, too, and how I got stuck in the infantry. Clausen wasn't a bad guy, for a Hun (1982, pp. 27-28).

By December Dunn managed a transfer into the RAF by making his 160 hours of private flying time look like 560. "Fed up with the infantry and lugging that damned three-inch mortar all over the countryside" (p. 30), Dunn seeks aerial combat, yet after his first hostile engagement in May is so shaken that he wonders if he could "get a transfer back to the infantry somehow" (p. 52). But like a thrown rider he gets back into the air next day and talks himself into persevering. From there he would go on to be the first Eagle to shoot down a German plane and the first American ace of World War II, claims that were established two wars later when Dunn was serving in Vietnam.

Before the war Bill Dunn had been an honest-to-goodness cowboy, rounding up wild horses in Montana and Wyoming; his descriptions of cutting out mustangs read like subsequent accounts of dogfights with Messerschmitts. Dixie Alexander's background is equally colorful, as a professional boxer (middleweight) and baseball player (in the Cincinnati Redlegs' minor league system). The romance of achievement in wartime skies prompted him to enlist in the U.S. Army Air Corps, but in the fall of 1939 prospective pilots needed two years of college, and so he found himself turned away. But rather than wait for American involvement, a draft notice, and no choice of service, Alexander left for Canada and the RCAF in October 1940. As noted, Dunn's narrative is filled with imagery from the Wild West; Dixie Alexander at times seems even more generically American, lacking Bill Dunn's career militarism and possessing instead an individualism that resists too much collective order. Why he chose to serve sums up the general motivation of many Eagles. Unlike the Flying Tigers of the American Volunteer Group (AVG) in China, these men were not service personnel; indeed, many were washouts or rejects. Nor did they fight for the high pay (including bonuses for combat kills) that made AVG work financially attractive; by American standards, RAF earnings were virtually nothing. True, they all had the flying bug and were attracted by what the British offered in the Hurricane and Spitfire, the hottest planes in the world. Affinities of culture and language made Britain seem a natural ally, with underdog status to match. By the time he joined No. 133 Eagle Squadron and began flying from Biggin Hill, one of the busiest and most famous RAF stations, Alexander could put his decision in perspective, speaking not just for himself but with his squadron colleagues in mind:

> We were not soldiers of fortune, but we were certainly adventurers, off to win the War for a noble cause, while having a great deal of fun and recognition. Few of us had a deep feeling of hatred for the Germans; we had experienced no physical contact with them. It was simply a continuation of W.W. I, and the Germans became natural adversaries. We were the "good guys," and they were the "bad guys." We were all fatalistic to some degree, and this can be a substitute for religion in itself. I think most of us believed that we would probably be killed before the end of the War—but never today, never tomorrow. It was a reckless kind of false courage, bordering a bit on the suicidal. The German pilots shared it too, along with their love for the fatherland, and the belief in their cause. A lot of us were loners, and that probably accounted in part for our decisions to come to England. We were headstrong young men, capable of making decisions (1988, p. 90).

As rejects or washouts, Alexander's style of volunteers thus had special motivation. And it wasn't just the glamour of flying Battle of Britain fighters; as transport pilot J. Gen Genovese reports in his *We Flew Without Guns* (1945), the crushing blow of failing his advanced training checkride at Randolph Field kept him from waiting until American involvement made his services more needed. "But the Army washed me out," he tells a friend trying to talk him out of volunteering for Britain. "They say I'm a dangerous flier" (p. 37).

Were the Eagles a bit reckless? Their memoirs abound in examples of daring and misbehavior well beyond the bounds of RAF standards. Plenty of British pilots had done their share of station beat-ups and flying under bridges, but only Dixie Alexander planned and practiced for doing such to the Arc de Triomphe on Armistice Day, 1942, intending to drop an American flag in the process—a wild design approved and underway at every level until by accident news of it reached RAF Fighter Command, where "all hell broke loose" (1988, p. 116) at the prospect of such an act.

In *The Eagles' War* Vern Haugland tells of Eagle pilot Jimmy Clark running an approaching RAF transport plane through a terrifying set of mock attacks, unmindful of the fact that its passenger was the dour, tail-coated Undersecretary for Air Harold Balfour, whose rage when dressing down the guilty pilot resembled that of "old Satan personified" (1992, p. 137). No American ever paid gross disrespect to figures of authority, but a certain classless exuberance would occasionally take its toll. The most dicey occasions were with royalty, when unintended accidents could happen. The worst RAF lore could offer was the tale of recently commissioned Ginger Lacey (a sergeant-pilot hero of the Battle of Britain) being recognized by a visiting King George VI and, to the horror of everyone else in the officers' mess, offering the king a beer (which, to his credit, the monarch kindly accepted). In *We Flew Without Guns* Gen Genovese tops that easily, telling how the presence of an unconscionably self-taken King Peter of Yugoslavia at an otherwise low-keyed meeting with King George and Queen Elizabeth drove a squadron mate to pretend he didn't know who George VI was. That the king took it well, Genovese reports, was due to the culprit's sense of being "completely natural and unaffected, and the combination of Americanism with that kind of honest naturalness is bound, particularly in a place like England, to result in a lot of humor" (1945, p. 58). As for the frustrations of having to handle the little details of life in an English rather than an American way, even someone as cosmopolitan as Jim Goodson learns to accept this good advice: "The secret of enjoying life in this country is never to be in a hurry. If you push them, they resent it. It's kind of like an Old Folks Home" (1983, p. 60).

More admirable are the signs of American ingenuity that emerge amid these highjinks. In *Fighter Pilot* Bill Dunn shoots off his mouth about how the London balloon barrage didn't seem to him like much of a deterrence. Challenged by a five-pound bet, he finds himself having to negotiate it with every inch of airspace apparently obstructed. That his life may be endangered is a serious matter, but even more compelling is the fact that a considerable store of side bets are riding with him. For Dunn, pragmatic logic saves the day: reasoning that train traffic must make it impossible for the Balloon Corps people to mount cables between the rails, he crosses "the whole city of London—east to west—no sweat" (1982, p. 64) by following the trackways at almost zero altitude. This beat-up of the world's largest town wins the bet and also gets him confined to barracks for a week; but the Air Ministry learns a valuable lesson and orders adjustments in the balloon dispersal "to close this previously unrecognized gap" (p. 65). Similar good comes from another royal encounter where tighter types feared for breaches of decorum, as Jim Goodson describes in *Tumult in the Clouds*: how King George visited the Eagles at RAF Debden, asked politely if "everything was all right," and was answered by a Texan that things would be better if he could wear cowboy boots with his uniform—with the surprising result that King's Rules and Regulations were amended to approve "the wearing of Texas boots with RAF officers' uniform by Texas pilots, providing they were black and without decoration" (1983, p. 65). Successful in this case, unsuccessful when it came to buzzing the Arc de Triomphe with the stars and stripes fluttering, American attitudes were the same: what was the harm in asking?

These accounts share one important aspect with conventional RAF narratives, and that is the gravity of war. On the day Art Donahue arrives at Kenley, the station is attacked. Amid the bombs and antiaircraft fire, this farm boy and civilian flight instructor who'd been in the military for less than two months suddenly realizes that this is "the first time I had ever seen an attempt to take a human life" (1941, p. 23). Within minutes he is seeing more, including a Ju-88 shot down, three of its crew members bailing out successfully with a fourth found near the crash, "The rip-cord by which he could have opened his parachute . . . severed by a bullet" (p. 25). When later on in *Tally-Ho!* the novice flyer sends an adversary down in flames to an almost certainly fatal crash, he must confess that "the realization of what I'd done awed me a little" (p. 186). On the other hand, careerist Bill Dunn musters similar candor to admit the unfashionable sentiment that, after shooting down and witnessing the death of his first enemy pilot, "To be truthful, I was elated—elated that I'd shot the bastard down before he could shoot me down" (1982, p. 57). In *War Eagles*, his contemporary account of the first American pilots in action, Col. James Saxon Childers tells of Gus Daymond and squadron-mate Chesley Peterson's English bride horsing around at a garden tea party "like any other pair of youngsters full of life and playing" (1943, p. 1). He then adds that less than twenty-four hours before Daymond has been over France on a fighter sweep, as the flyer himself pauses to describe:

> The whole squadron went over to shoot up whatever we could find. We went in low, just over the treetops, and I found this alcohol factory and flew round it a couple of times firing at condensation coils with my cannons and sort of blasted hell out of it, until brown smoke was pouring out and I knew it was finished. Then I flew on toward the coast and saw a man with a surveying instrument in a field, but when I was about to push the button I saw he was a defenseless man without a gun of any kind, so I

thought I'd let him live and I did. Then I flew on out, and I saw about fifteen men in a gun emplacement. I was flying low and coming at them from behind, and they didn't see me, and I opened with everything at three hundred yards. I flew straight at them firing everything until I was almost in amongst them, and arms and legs and heads and legs were flying every which-a-way. There was one body that sort of leapt up into the air and looped the loop and the head went sailing off in the other direction. I reckon I shot that fellow up into a lot of pieces, all right. Then I flew on out over the Channel and came on home (p. 2).

"That was yesterday afternoon?" Childers asks for confirmation; Daymond answers "Yes" and turns back to his horse-play on the lawn. Having lived and worked with No. 71 Eagle Squadron as he did, Colonel Childers can only wonder at this immediate, day-to-day contrast between peace and war, just as Art Donahue had recognized when being dropped so suddenly into the midst of the Battle of Britain.

Later on in *War Eagles* Daymond is quoted again, thrilled at his first kill but confused and remorseful as "I realized that I'd shot a plane and shot a man, and I was thinking about the poor guy being in trouble" (p. 33). As he pauses to watch, hoping that the German pilot will bail out, Daymond is nearly killed himself by another Messerschmitt on his tail. And so the lesson is quickly learned, enabling the style of discourse that's meant to be so shocking at the start.

With distance, attitudes toward adversaries soften. It is a rubric of RAF storytelling that while aircrew members of Bomber Command have sympathy for their victims right from the start, their Fighter Command counterparts experience distinct stages of response: at the time identifying with their adversaries most generously only as technological opponents, then after the war in terms of sport, and only in the long view of memory as human beings like themselves. *War Eagles* captures this first stage when Colonel Childers asks the squadron medical officer "what he thought it meant to the boys to shoot down other boys" and is told it means "no more to them than shooting ducks in a shooting gallery." Hardly ever driven by hate, their hunting is almost purely a test of skill, pitting one machine against another: "I've had them tell me," the medical officer confides, "they sort of jumped and caught their breath as a Hun pilot bailed out of a blazing aircraft; they had quite forgotten there was anybody inside" (pp. 242-43). The joy is in accomplishment of technique. As the squadron intelligence officer reports, he loves to write the five Eagle pilots held in prisoner-of-war camps long letters whenever the squadron downs another plane, "giving the details of the fight and telling just how Jerry got his behind shot off" simply to tweak the German censors (p. 321).

As expected, adversarial relationships take on a human dimension when one's opponent is recognized as a human being. Leo Nomis, having volunteered for hard duty on Malta, recalls just such an episode for Vern Haugland in *The Eagles' War* when finding himself locked in formation with a Messerschmitt, unable to risk a break because his cannon and machine guns are jammed. In such a circumstance, perception is suddenly clarified well beyond the obstructions of battle:

> My first impulse was to turn away, but I had an instant realization that this would be fatal. The 109 pilot had evidently resolved this also, because I could see him fanning his rudder in an attempt to slow down more quickly and drop behind or under me.
>
> Even then, at the verge of panic, I remember registering the extreme clarity and beauty of the scene, incongruous as it was—the enemy plane, the yellow nose etched perfectly against the dark blue of the sea below. I remember staring fascinated for a second at the number 24 on the 109 fuselage.
>
> I was slowing down the Spit to keep pace with him, and at the same time fighting the urge to panic. It was at this point, when our wingtips were literally together, that the brilliant idea struck me. I could make an appeal to chivalry.
>
> Our gazes at each other had never faltered since the beginning of the predicament. We could see only each other's eyes; he wore a mask, and I did too. So, in a motion which I considered should explain everything—remember, he had a cockpit canopy, but mine was open, so every movement must have been perfectly clear—I pointed dramatically down at the port wing cannon with a gloved finger, then raised the finger and drew it across my throat. This, I figured, would indicate that my guns were jammed and therefore mercy could be accorded me (1992, p. 102).

The German pilot breaks away, becoming "a miniature against the seascape by the time I could follow him with my eyes." Nomis wonders if this is indeed evidence of good sportsmanship or whether his adversary has misinterpreted the gesture as a threat, but in either event war can be said to have stopped for a moment, giving time for both description and communication.

Because Bill Dunn's career reached from the universally admired heroics of the Battle of Britain to the controversies of America's war in Vietnam, his words for the enemy are rigorously unsentimental. Yet early in *Fighter Pilot* he reports an isolated incident where a student pilot finds himself wing to wing with a Messerschmitt 110. "With the bejesus scared out of him," as Dunn puts it, the student waits to be killed ingloriously at the controls of his dinky, unarmed Miles Master. Instead, the Me-110 crew waves, "as if to say 'See you when you learn to fly,'" and banks away. "Not all enemy airmen were as gallant" (1982, p. 33), Dunn regrets, but the point is made. Elsewhere this Eagle pilot laughs about how a squadron mate who'd studied German in college would get on a Messerschmitt Staffel's radio frequency and mock their own "jabbering" (p. 65), and even when shot down and floating in a waterlogged dinghy he can maintain a humorously feisty attitude when buzzed by the enemy: "I suppose it was the son of a bitch who had shot me down. He waggled his wings at me, I thumbed my nose at him" (p. 73). In the rescue launch that picks him up are three other RAF pilots plus two Luftwaffe flyers also fished from the Channel. With the rum provided, each group toasts the other's luck in being saved; one toast follows another until all six are enjoying a roaring good fellowship. "Poor bastards," Dunn reflects when on shore the military police take their prisoners away. "They weren't such bad guys after all and about our same age. The six of us pilots could really have turned one on that evening, if the stiff-necked MP officer had let our two Hun buddies join us at a local pub to celebrate our miraculous escape from the briny deep" (p. 75). Near war's end, when the Eagle veteran is flying with the 406th Fighter Group from France, he searches a barn and finds the bodies of two very young German soldiers laid out to look like children asleep. "What a bloody awful crime against humanity war is," Dunn laments. But only for a moment, because the farmer warns him the angelic-looking bodies have been positioned this way for a reason: they are booby-trapped. "Wouldn't you know some Kraut son-of-a-bitch would do something like that, the bastards," Dunn concludes (p. 151).

Of all the Eagles and former Eagles, Dixie Alexander tells the most intimate stories of what his Luftwaffe adversaries were like. His advantage is meeting them on neutral ground, in Portugal, where mechanical problems have forced him to land while transferring with a flight of P-39s to North Africa. Here he finds himself sharing a hotel floor with staff from the Japanese legation, but as he and the Allied flyers with him wait for the American Embassy to get them out, they encounter people even more interesting:

> One day we discovered a new bar and I was engaged in conversa-
> tion by a young fellow who obviously was not Portuguese, but

spoke English well. It didn't take long to find out that we were
both in the same fix. He was an interned Luftwaffe pilot. There
were a number of them in Lisbon, under almost the same circumstances as Allied pilots. In the ensuing days we met all of
them and, surprisingly, got on well. For the most part, their
gripes, likes and dislikes were much the same as ours. We were
pilots. We avoided political discussion and loyalties by mutual
consent and contented ourselves with talking about combat, aircraft, girls, and other subjects normal to young pilots. While
never completely friends, we were good associates in our own
way, enjoyed each other's company and stood as a united front
in our bar against the general public. How true this friendship
was, and how highly the Luftwaffe boys valued it, I was soon to
learn (1988, p. 134).

Friendship's payoff comes when plans are made to send Dixie
and nine other Allied airmen by ship to Gibraltar. To their surprise,
they learn about it from the Germans even before the American Embassy clues them in. The Germans have heard the matter being discussed at their own embassy, where the details were intercepted and
plans laid to bomb—a legitimate act because Dixie and his colleagues
would be traveling to an active theater for service against the Reich.

Wasn't this dangerous for the Germans to tip Dixie off? His Luftwaffe pal says that "they had discussed it, and felt it was their duty
as kindred souls and pilot officers to inform us; that we deserved a
death in the air, rather than what was in store for us" (p. 135). Re-
fusing to board wins Dixie and his friends some prison time in Lisbon
and, after their eventual safe removal to North Africa, a court martial
for treason. Happily, the judicial affair is just a formality, with almost
no penalty (two weeks' confinement to base, but not to conflict with
flying duties). Thanks to the higher loyalty of their German friends,
they are alive to serve out this minimal confinement; in the meantime
a Portuguese officer has told them that the ship in question was
indeed bombed and sunk.

Dixie Alexander's adversaries knew very well what brought him
to Portugal: he was forced down not in retreat from hostile action
but in search of it, transferring from what had become a quieter air
war over England to the immensely more active desert conflict in
North Africa. It is during another such transfer that Art Donahue reveals his own sympathy for those he must oppose—even as he, like
Dixie will a year later, leaves a quieter England to volunteer for a
harder fight elsewhere. The time is 25 December 1941; the place,
Gibraltar, where Donahue is with some other RAF pilots en route to
God knows where—ostensibly to Cairo, although perhaps to Malta,

and in fact to Singapore where the Japanese assault has just begun. The moment is a transition point between *Tally-Ho!* and *Last Flight from Singapore*, and therefore isn't discussed in much detail in either book. But in Vern Haugland's *The Eagle Squadrons*, No. 121 Eagle Squadron veteran John A. Campbell, who was also making the transfer, tells of Donahue's circumstance.

"Christmas of 1941 was a bad time for Art," Campbell recalls. "It was the first chance he had for a lot of time to think about what the war meant to the parents of fighter pilots on both sides. He said he felt like weeping for the mothers of the German airmen he had killed" (1979, p. 120). Yet even as he weeps Art Donahue is off to kill more airmen; before *Last Flight from Singapore* concludes, he finds himself machine-gunning tightly packed boatloads of Japanese infantry troops as well. Although mindful that unlike German soldiers he had strafed over France these troops have neither shelter or anywhere to "scatter or throw themselves flat or do anything except just sit up and take it" (1943, p. 140), he finds it easy to rake the target with fire; "There's nothing to it, really—you just press in with your thumb. There was the abrupt shattering roar from the guns in my wings and then eight ghostly white tracers snaking ahead eagerly, toward the boat and its helpless passengers. They would know nothing more" (p. 141). When the boat's solitary gunner wounds Donahue in return, it seems only fair; the only thing "awful" he finds about the experience is having to fight for consciousness while bringing his plane back (p. 142). No joy in killing, no recrimination in being shot—such is the professionalism that lets even a sensitive idealist fight as he must. Adversaries are just that: opponents to be faced as technologies and abilities provide. It is in just such a test of his abilities that Art Donahue dies a year and a half later back in England, where on patrol duties once again he discerns a Luftwaffe intruder's pattern and heads out next day for a planned interception, one from which he does not return.

Eagle narratives, then, brought readers the first descriptions of what the American air war over England, the Channel, and Europe had been like. There was plenty of fulsome description of how romantic things looked to young Americans fresh from the States. Whether their homes were in Los Angeles or rural Minnesota, few had seen the likes of hedgerows, thatched cottages, and quaint village pubs that characterized the countryside where RAF stations nestled among the hop fields of Kent or the beauty of Cumberland. Here was a storybook land, and for now the stories would be theirs. Noting that his first base took its name from the nearby village of

Crosby-on-Eden, Jim Goodson pauses in *Tumult in the Clouds* to exclaim "And Eden it was." He can also counsel his reader that "If you've never strolled out of The Dog and Gun into a glorious summer evening, hand in hand with a doe-eyed WAAF through the beautiful lush countryside of Crosby-on-Eden, then, my poor friend, you have never really lived!" (1983, p. 52). Yet such Edens could stir themselves quickly into the mix of modern battle, especially when two squadrons shared the same station and scrambled directly from their dispersal pens to intercept a Luftwaffe raid, as Bill Dunn recounts in *Fighter Pilot*: "The excitement of the moment," he writes, "reached its absolute peak when you launched out of your bay and went blasting at full throttle across the grass and there, roaring almost head-on toward you, came some sod who was being scrambled from the opposite side of the airfield." Getting airborne in less than two minutes was a dangerous necessity. "Some near misses and some prangs did occur," Dunn recalls, "but not as often as you would think" (1982, p. 50).

Then there are the aerial engagements themselves, initially vast confrontations that in a moment break up into what James Saxon Childers describes in *War Eagles* as a dozen individual fights, "planes whirling around and around in pursuit of each other, moving so rapidly that they looked from above almost like hoops rolling through the sky, until suddenly one part of the hoop would explode or burst into flames," while another might break away and dive, "its camouflaged wings and fuselage almost instantly merging into the landscape as it went down" (1943, p. 266). In *The Eagles' War* Howard "Deac" Hively tells Vern Haugland how when he took to the silk after an engine fire "I did not pop out, but seemed to float up over my airplane and just hang there," watching straps hanging up and his helmet still dangling from its radio cord. To his amazement, he counts seven bullet holes in his plane's right wing and is "quite concerned, for I had not been aware that any enemy plane had come close" (1992, p. 201). In this same volume Leo Nomis watches a Spitfire explode, shedding a wing and disgorging its pilot, the body of which falls before him as in "a film unfolding before me in a cinema." Almost forty years afterwards, Nomis's "clearest memory" of that event "is that the body seemed to be leaving a trail of papers in its wake as it fell away and became smaller and smaller. Probably, these were maps and charts that had been tucked into the man's boots" (p. 106). No parachute is seen to open.

For one of the Eagles' biggest engagements, Barry Mahon has a front-row seat (as recounted in Haugland's *The Eagle Squadrons*), afloat in a dinghy just beyond the harbor at Dieppe during the experimental landing exercise of Operation Jubilee on 19 August 1942. Shot down by the wingman of a Focke-Wulf 190 he has just downed himself, Mahon finds himself just two and one-half minutes later looking up at where he's been:

> I lay on my back in the dinghy and watched the tremendous air battle, probably the greatest air show the world had yet seen. There must have been 80 or 90 German planes and an equal number of British aircraft in a five-miles-square cube of the sky.
>
> The sights that morning and part of the afternoon were unbelievable. There would be a Spit being chased by a German being chased by a Spit being chased by a German, and the first three would be blown up, leaving the remaining one victorious until he turned into the guns of another opponent.
>
> As a matter of fact, after the adrenalin level of my blood went down I found the spectacle fascinating—a giant Fourth of July display, only much more ominous. The spent bullets were falling like hailstones, so hot they made sizzling noises as they struck the water (1979, p. 154).

As fate has it, 19 August is no Fourth of July for Mahon, who drifts to shore and is captured. Yet his luck survives, for as his German captors prepare to march him and several thousand Allied infantrymen he recognizes the route as one he himself was scheduled to strafe that afternoon. At first skeptical, the Wehrmacht officer in charge believes him when the first No. 121 Eagle Squadron Spitfire appears. After that, Mahon's maps get the prisoners transported safely.

That the Eagle squadrons were still flying within the RAF as late as Operation Jubilee speaks for both the complexity and paradox of their roles. Over eight months earlier squadron personnel had been asleep or drowsily listening to the late BBC news when the Japanese attack on Pearl Harbor was announced. Chesley Peterson, a charter member of No. 71 Eagle Squadron and now its leader, had to be awakened by the intelligence officer; yet by the time he reached the mess there was virtual pandemonium at hand, as liquor flowed while American and British pilots toasted their now official alliance. But there were serious intentions afoot as well. "I never saw the Eagles so hopped up and full of fight in my life" (1991, p. 168), Peterson reports to researcher Philip D. Caine in *Eagles of the RAF*.

Next morning, representatives from Nos. 71 and 121 Eagle squadrons met at the American Embassy in London; No. 133 Eagle Squadron was too far away, training in Northern Ireland, or it would have sent officers too. The intention was to volunteer their services en masse to the lately renamed United States Army Air Force—a strategy that was patriotic but also pragmatic, as the squadrons had developed their own group style of fighting and wished to keep it intact for what would now be an obviously long haul against both Germany and Japan. As Ambassador John Winant phoned their wishes to the White House, delegates from No. 121 Eagle standing nearby could overhear President Roosevelt's answer: that the Eagles would be transferred as soon as possible. But when weeks passed with no likelihood for movement in evidence, Peterson took another step and petitioned Fighter Command for an immediate unit transfer to Singapore, where the Eagles could remain in the RAF and fight America's Japanese enemies as well. Fighter Command's answer, voiced by Air Chief Marshal Sholto Douglas, was at least unambiguous: Singapore was on its last legs and wasn't worth a squadron. The Eagles would stay in Great Britain.

One American pilot, however, was presently en route there: Art Donahue, who gets the news at Gibraltar where his regular RAF contingent is awaiting transfer East. His reaction sets the tone of seriousness that characterizes so much of *Last Flight from Singapore*:

> I felt dazed and overwhelmed. After all the fighting that we Americans in the RAF had been through, believing that we were helping to make this unnecessary, it had come at last, all in a twinkling, and our country was committed to take part in the slaughter.
>
> In the Wardroom we drank a toast with the British officers, to our new alliance. Then later, at midnight, we gathered around the radio to listen to detail after terrible detail of the world-shaking events that had happened in the last few hours.
>
> Everyone was subdued—we Americans because of the tragedy it spelled for our country, and the others because we felt it would lengthen the war to have Japan added to our enemies. The only bright side for us Americans was knowing that we wouldn't be outlaws any more in the eyes of our own country—as we were when I went home on leave to the States the previous winter and wasn't allowed to wear my uniform (1943, p. 18).

This is the sort of thoughtfulness that distinguished Art Donahue from some of his more boisterous Eagle colleagues; given the contrast between his somber reaction in Gibraltar and the whoop-and-holler doings among No. 71 Eagle Squadron at North Weald, his disinclination to stay among his fellow Americans can be understood. Yet as 8 December dawns, it is to their desired destination of Singapore that he's already traveling, forever one step ahead.

The eighth of December is also an interesting day for Dixie Alexander. As a sergeant pilot he's been excluded from the riotous behavior in the officers' mess, and in fact doesn't learn of Pearl Harbor until at breakfast the following morning. His first thoughts are American losses, but those worries are moderated by the fact that "there would be no further doubt about America's position in the War." Here is where *They Called Me Dixie* takes a critical turn, as the author's use of the personal pronoun reveals a noteworthy sense of identification. "We knew we had just gained a very powerful ally," he writes, "and that in itself was reason to rejoice. We no longer stood alone" (1988, pp. 69-70). Dixie's sentiment confirms what Hubert L. "Bert" Stewart tells Philip D. Caine in *Eagles of the RAF*, that in the heavy action of the months before "England's war had become the Eagles' war and all the Eagles were focused on the survival of the United Kingdom with little thought of much else" (1991, p. 167). Perhaps this is why the clear-headed thoughts of a sergeant pilot like Alexander ring more true than the party-fueled bluster of some commissioned officers, and why even those most outspoken about wanting to rush off and fight the Japanese soon settled down and resumed their RAF duties, flying fighter sweeps from England in preparation for Dieppe.

When the Eagles did officially transfer, it was on 29 September 1942, and into the Fourth Fighter Group of the Eighth Air Force, an aggregation that stayed right there in England from where the war could be taken into Germany. With the three Eagle squadrons standing together for the first time, their ranks watched the Union Jack come down at RAF Debden and the Stars and Stripes replace it. Air Chief Marshal Sholto Douglas thanked them for their service before Maj. Gen. Carl Spaatz and Brig. Gen. Frank Hunter welcomed them into the USAAF. There were things the Eagles preferred not to give up, and so they didn't: regulations were amended to let them wear their RAF wings together with their USAAF wings, left breast and right, and for the time being they could keep their beloved Spitfires, roundels painted over with the U.S. star. For the time being, their units stayed together. But the fledgling Eighth Air Force had a desperate need for combat-experienced pilots, and in time the Eagles found themselves dispersed, many to assume leadership positions in this peacetime air force so suddenly thrust into war.

Not every Eagle transferred. Bill Dunn elected to stay in the RAF and was given command of an RCAF squadron; not until 15 June 1943 was the USAAF able to "come and get me," as he puts it in *Fighter Pilot*, a consequence of the British government having "agreed on sort of a reverse lend-lease arrangement" (1982, p. 111) for holdouts such as himself: combat trained by the British as he was, the United States would pay a hefty sum to get him back to instruct American cadets. Yet even those who did, which included almost all of the Eagles still alive and flying, gave pause to James Saxon Childers, who in *War Eagles* describes the transfer ceremony and its aftermath in what continued to look like and be treated like a Battle of Britain heroes' flying club:

> And what of the future? Could lieutenants, captains, and majors in the United States Army shoot flares out of windows and sky-rockets up the chimney of the officers' mess?
>
> All that afternoon and that night the rain fell, until the roads were terribly slippery. Because of the slippery roads the air-drome fire department was a trifle late, sometime after midnight, in arriving to save the officers' mess.
>
> Unknown persons had shot flares out of windows and skyrockets up the chimney, and had tossed smoke bombs into a few odd corners.
>
> While members of the fire department were debating with lieutenants, captains, and majors the wisdom of burning down "the whole bloody place," Robbie [No. 71 Eagle Squadron's intelligence officer, J. Roland Robinson] was broadcasting to England and to America a farewell to the Eagles:
>
> "The sky was full of planes returning from battle over France. The ground crews, who had seen so many pilots fly away for battle, were looking at the sky and counting" (1943, pp. 332-33).

And so with Wing Commander Robinson, Member of Parliament and the future Lord Martonmere, shaping their public image to the last, the American Eagle squadrons celebrated their way into American military service, something that for many of them would have been unimaginable just two years before. Needless to say, the U.S. Army Air Force would never be the same.

Chapter 2

Fighter Jocks

AT THE END OF September 1942—after nearly two years as members of the RAF—the Eagle squadrons not only joined the United States Army Air Force but became the nucleus of what would become its key pursuit unit, the Fourth Fighter Group. The legacy these Eagle pilots brought with them is apparent in the preciously few words devoted to the units by their respective chief commanders, Air Chief Marshal Sholto Douglas and Gen. Henry H. Arnold. Of the 1,400 pages that comprise their memoirs, Douglas gives the Eagles two pages, Arnold three. And of the little they say, the greater part is devoted to these squadrons' misbehavior.

"Right from the beginning I had heard rumors from the R.A.F. station where the Americans were working up their first Eagle Squadron to an operational status that they were a pretty wild lot," Douglas confides in *Combat and Command* (1966). Learning that the station commander's method of "dealing with the frisky new-comers was to reach and take them by the scruff of their necks and bang their heads together," he approves. "I recalled my own experiences in coping with the exuberance of the Americans when I had them serving under me in my squadrons in the first war, and I knew that that was just the sort of treatment that they understood. It got results, and that was what mattered" (p. 474). Arnold sees the problem more psychologically, remarking in *Global Misson* (1949) that "The British had some trouble with them—too many prima donnas" (p. 219). Arnold should have known that this was how his RAF counterpart viewed him! In tandem with Douglas's comments on the Eagle squadrons is his dismay at Arnold's conduct during their visit to a more active RAF unit, No. 601 Squadron, in April 1941, while the United States was still outside the war:

> When we got to the operations room [after a scramble], Arnold shook everybody by asking if he could speak to the squadron over the radio as they went about their patrol. I agreed, and Arnold said a few crisp words of thanks and good wishes. As I listened I wondered what the Germans, who monitored all our radio communications, would make of that, and if it would dawn upon them that the voice that had come up on the radio was none other than from the chief of the then still neutral American Air Force (1966, p. 474).

With these precedents it is no wonder that the Fourth Fighter Group and subsequent units would cultivate a style of flamboyance that distinguished them from more traditional modes of conduct in war. Of course, the RAF itself had established several distinguishing factors. Fighter pilots, for example, would leave the top button of their battle dress undone, even on the ground, as a symbol of the type of work they did. In the air, silk scarves had replaced service ties in the interest of keeping a better lookout, but bomber crews soon added scarves to their military dress, the more colorful the better. Throughout the war flyers alone, of all U.K. servicemen, dined on bacon and eggs before fighting. But what American fighter pilots brought to the air war being mounted from England was something else indeed.

Helping them along was the fact that they were coming in from the outside. But as the wartime saying put it, coming from America to be "over here" brought with it extravagances of pay, food, and sexuality that took serial importance in popular legend along with their simple presence.

Most disconcerting to the British was the typically American sense of individualism. There were no distinctions based on class, such as determined which Englishmen would be RAF officers and which sergeant pilots; by 1942 the old Army Air Corps requirement of two years' college, minimal as that was, had been dropped. Promotions came quickly, with twenty-five-year-old lieutenant colonels not uncommon once the Fourth Fighter Group got up to speed. B-17s flew more visibly than did RAF Halifaxes and Lancasters, in the daylight and in huge formations. American fighter squadrons were bigger, noisier, and more centralized, their aggressiveness given unofficial but widespread recognition in the person of five-victory aces, a concept that did not exist in the Royal Air Force.

Situationally, there was even realistic justification for such contrasting attitudes. Unlike the English, who had been fighting a defensive war from and above their own homes, the Americans were visitors to the battle, coming into town like hired gunslingers to save the day, clean things up, then head back to the faraway place they'd come from. Therefore it should not be surprising that these American airmen acted more like Butch Cassidy and the Sundance Kid than Churchill's oratorically stylized Arthurian few.

The three Eagle squadrons were the first members of the Fourth Fighter Group. Soon, the group's staffing would come from the cadet training program of the United States Army Air Force. The story of one flyer caught in-between, John T. Godfrey, highlights the transition. Neither an Eagle nor a USAAF recruit, he created an identity for himself that became, if not a model, a precedent for a style of behavior that would reflect the group's image. *The Look of Eagles* (1958) is his autobiography—written in the thirteenth year after the war as he fought a losing but heroic battle with amyotrophic lateral sclerosis, a disease often associated with its most famous (and seemingly indefatigable) victim, baseball star Lou Gehrig. Godfrey's candor and seriousness, in the context of his terminal illness, gives his narrative a special authenticity, one that makes the nature of his Air Force actions all the more remarkable.

As a high school graduate in June 1941, Godfrey worries that he will miss the excitement of World War II because the Army Air Corps deems him unworthy. The two-year college requirement sends him north to the Royal Canadian Air Force, the route of so many of his predecessors. By November he's in England for Advanced Flight Training School, ranked as a sergeant but in line for an officer's commission. Here is where his limitations of character continue working their magic. It was "the monotonous humdrum of work" (p. 20) rather than any patriotic idealism that had prompted him to go off to war; now, on a similar lark, Godfrey reacts against the "monotonous" nature of his posting by going absent without leave (AWOL). But, as with his success at joining the RCAF, his bad behavior leads not to punishment but to reward. Prepared to remand him to a disciplinary course on military courtesy, Godfrey's commanding officer (CO) is perplexed by another paper that has appeared in the young man's file: a commission making him a pilot officer, effective before the date of his offense. "I cannot take disciplinary actions unless I conduct a special court," the CO advises. "In other words, you have buggered things up so much that it would take a week of paper work to straighten this mess out. I would consider it a personal favor if you would get the hell off my base!" (p. 37). Thus Godfrey is able to leave, congratulating himself on having entered the office as non-com on charge and leaving it as a freshly promoted officer.

Godfrey's flying career continues with just such rewards for misbehavior, from sassing a commander over his pet dog to abandoning formation in pursuit of German fighters. Such extravagances became a hallmark of American behavior—if not in actual fact, then in frequency of widely told stories. Both Richard Turner in *Big Friend, Little Friend* (1969) and James H. Howard in *Roar of the Tiger* (1991) recall with relish the last grand gesture of George "Stud" Hall, "one of the most popular fun-loving characters you could hope to meet," as Howard attests (1991, p. 268). Turner seconds Howard in reporting how "while going down over Germany Stud was reeling off a list of debts owed to friends before bailing out. Whether true or not, it was just the kind of stunt Stud would have pulled in the face of danger and death" (1969, p. 73).

Other tales of bravado wind up on notes of tactical success. Forced to land in Portugal while en route from England to North Africa, Jack Ilfrey lets those who would intern him refuel his P-38 and accept his instructions on how to start it. Yet as he explains in *Happy Jack's Go-Buggy* (1979), these courtesies are not for his captors' benefit. Instead, he revs the engine, blows the observing Portuguese pilot off the wing, and takes off to resume his journey (p. 73). In *Thunderbolt* (1982), Marvin Bledsoe transforms a V-1 launching site mission into a happy hunting grounds for trucks and locomotives. "We were finding so many targets because our fighter planes hadn't dared come down on the deck in this heavily protected area along the coast," he reports. "We were there only by accident, because some politician had hollered for somebody to do something about those buzz bombs" (p. 180). John Godfrey, already notorious for breaking ranks (yet shooting down Messerschmitts in the process), spoils a carefully planned attack by calling a premature bounce on a group of Focke-Wulfs—but merits an excuse because this action drives the FW-190s away from the bombers, almost certainly saving losses (1958, p. 123).

Then there is the stuff of war movies. Shot down and hiding out among the French while drafting his memoir, *Fighter Pilot* (1946), L.C. Beck, Jr., recalls the loss of a comrade just a month before. Shooting up gun positions in the D-day invasion area, the pilot is able to make one last transmission to his wingman. "Benny must have been hit badly," Beck imagines, "probably a 20mm right in the gut or something of the like. He managed to say, 'Eddie, I'm hit.' He then turned straight into the gun which had gotten him, and with a death grip on the trigger he flew his ship directly into the gun emplacement—firing all the way. He never intended pulling up and with a last bit of effort had gone out; the way only a truly great 'Fighter Pilot' would" (p. 97). The image may be projected in the language of B-movies and war comic books, but the impulse is authentic, at least as Beck perceives it. Such is his instinctive spirit of aggression on the first morning in hiding when he wakes to see a staffel of FW-190s passing overhead: "My blood began to tingle and I had a maddening desire to shoot them" (p. 53).

Although Beck's responses are necessarily fantasies, they correspond to real actions by his colleagues. Maj. James Howard found thirty Messerschmitts attacking a flight of bombers and took them on himself, shooting down three and driving the rest away—an act he tried to keep quiet but which won him the reputation of being a "one-man Air Force" and a recommendation for the Congressional Medal of Honor. Many fighter pilots, albeit with support, shot down even more, and Lt. Chuck Yeager became the first to destroy five or more enemy planes in a single engagement, earning the title "ace in a day." Yeager's career became quite publicly heroic, and the way he fought the air war from England became the foundation for this myth. His autobiography and the several books in which his exploits are reported abound in flamboyant exploits, from his training in Nevada, daring escape from France after being shot down, and subsequent combat experiences to the way he and close friend Bud Anderson celebrated the end of their tours: swooping over Yeager's escape route, dropping their wing tanks on Mount Blanc and shooting them afire, and finally buzzing the Arc de Triomphe in Paris. Their only punishment for these infractions is the irony of having missed in the process their group's most successful day of fighting.

That the record of the Fourth Fighter Group and others in the Eighth Air Force amounts to more than just high risks, misbehavior, and shenanigans is due to the genius with which all this exuberant aggression was channeled. There was no real master plan for doing so; rather, it was the coincidence of these young men coming to fly and fight in just these conditions that allowed what could have been irresponsibility to be transformed into genuinely effective action. It was in the fall of 1942 that the nature of the war itself was changing, from defense to offense. With American involvement came a transformation of the war's character as well: from few to many, from small to large, and from scarcity to plenty. With a fighter group led by a lieutenant colonel unlikely to be a veteran careerist, service college or university trained, but rather likely to be a high school graduate just twenty-five or twenty-six years old, the nature of leadership altered, as did the style curried by the even younger men under their command. These youngsters cultivated a certain sense of swagger and cockiness, a mode of carrying themselves that would dominate the Air Force for half a century to come, that of the fighter jock. In fashioning an understanding of America's quest for space, Tom Wolfe saw that impulse directed to the stars, with Chuck Yeager himself setting the standard for competition and achievement that was needed to compel young men to risk being the highest and fastest of all; in this sense Wolfe's *The Right Stuff* (1979) is the final chapter in World War II fighter pilot history. But there would be no "right stuff" without the culturing of this raw behavior into a method of fighting that made American air action from England so successful.

Numbers and diversity served this channeling well. Within the Fourth Fighter Group, remnants of the Eagle squadrons sought to retain their RAF heritage, yielding a de facto competition between old and new. But in time the Fourth became just one of many fighter groups, and among them real competition was a defining element, along with the different personalities of their leaders (such as Hub Zemke and Don Blakeslee) and aircraft (the P-47 Thunderbolt and the P-51 Mustang, respectively). With Capt. Eddie Rickenbacker's World War I score of twenty-six kills as the goal, a race developed to see who would be the first modern fighter pilot to reach and eclipse it—a race in which the ambitions of flyers and the eagerness of newspaper reporters were mutually reinforcing.

The first factor in this tautly dramatic scheme was the change in aircraft. It was not just that the Eagle squadrons had flown Spitfires; for the first two years of war the Spitfire had been an icon for Britain and the Allies' struggle itself. The Eagles brought their Spitfires with them into the Fourth Fighter Group, and one of the first signs of change was the American star crudely painted over the British roundel on the sides and wings of each machine. In *Thunderbolt!* (1959) Robert S. Johnson describes how radically different were Spitfires and their replacements, the mighty P-47 Thunderbolts that changed how pilots would fly and fight. "The differences between our Thunderbolt and the Spitfire were amazing," he attests. "The P-47 was a giant, a massive weapon with a tremendous roar and dynamite in each wing. Not so the English fighter, much smaller than the Thunderbolt, sleeker, almost like a lightweight fighter with the agility to dart in and out of battle with lithe, rapid movements" (p. 97). Clumsy at low altitude, the P-47 was a plane to swoop down from high altitude, make a quick pass, then outdive its opponent by virtue of its massive weight. It was also a brashly confrontational weapon, its hulking radial engine, air-cooled, providing a sturdy shield, as opposed to the Spitfire's vulnerable liquid-cooled Merlin. A true heavyweight, the Thunderbolt could absorb immense damage and still fly; pilots would return to count bullet holes and flak punctures in the hundreds, Johnson at one point comparing his battered aircraft to "a sieve" (p. 161).

Pilots trained in the Thunderbolt loved it. Those transitioning from the Spitfire felt just the opposite. In *The Eagles' War* Vern Haugland quotes Chesley Peterson's story about one of the early P-47 missions flown by former Eagles, a mission in which Peterson earns the Thunderbolt's first kill, a FW-190 that he outdives over Belgium. On the way home, however, the P-47's engine blows three cylinders and freezes up, forcing Peterson to ditch in the Channel. Retrieved by the air rescue service and returned to his base at Debden, he faces a special problem. "I had a difficult time," he confesses, "to a certain extent, because I had to tell my Group that I had been shot down. The P-47 was not a very popular aircraft in the Fourth Group at that time, and I could not possibly let them know that the engine had failed. Officially I had been shot down. It was several years before I finally told people that the trouble really had been engine failure" (1992, p. 155). No wonder, given that his pilots, homesick for their Spitfires, had taken to calling its unwanted replacement the "Repulsive Scatterbolt."

A more complex matter involved the introduction of the P-51 Mustang a year later. The first impression of almost every pilot who sees it is the same: that this new plane seems more like a Spitfire. And so, to some extent, it is: more lightly armed, more maneuverable, smaller and especially sleeker with its glycol-cooled engine. Above all, it was an *exciting* plane; John Godfrey describes himself and his squadron mates as being "queued up like housewives at a bargain sale" to see it (1958, p. 95). With its different flying characteristics, tactics once again changed; instead of bouncing Focke-Wulfs and Messerschmitts from above the bomber formations, the P-51 Mustangs would range ahead, clearing a path for the B-17 streams. This plane was a Spitfire *plus*, as Bud Anderson notes in *To Fly and Fight*

(1990): it could "do everything that the Spitfire could do—and better yet, could do it over Berlin" (p. 75).

The long-range Mustang came on line with the Eighth Air Force's new commander, Gen. Jimmy Doolittle. Doolittle's impera-. tive was to destroy the German air force wherever he could find it: being built in factories, assembled on air fields, or engaged in the air. It was the Mustang that made such aerial engagement a real possibility, but the new rules applied to Thunderbolts too. "All the German fighters were to be chased to their destruction, wherever they may be, wherever we could find them," P-47 ace Francis Gabreski recalls in *Gabby: A Fighter Pilot's Life* (1991). "Even more than that, we were told to strike anything we could see in Germany—airfields, staff cars, trucks, trains." Mustangs swept widely for their quarry; Thunderbolts, with their battering ram of an engine which the pilot could use as a shield, would complete their escort duties and sweep the deck. "That put a very different complexion on the whole war," Gabreski concludes, thinking of the race for high scores between pilots and especially among competing groups. "It became a real free-for-all" (p. 143).

An excellent contemporary record for the spirit of this numbers-chase is Eric Friedheim and Samuel W. Taylor's *Fighters Up* (1944). As American journalists living with the squadrons, these writers show a compulsion to make their stories as exciting as the air war itself. But rather than journalistic hype, their style reflects the enthusiasm and competition that was inherent in the Eighth Air Force ever since the Eagles transferred to form its initial fighter group. They relish such details as a squadron getting its first Mustangs and being so thrilled with the planes that instead of spending twenty or thirty hours in practice, as done when transitioning from Spitfires to Thunderbolts, the pilots take a fifteen-minute practice flight and then charge off in search of the enemy. And as for personifying quotes, the journalists are eager to report such characterizations as those made by Lt. Nicholas Megura, whose story has internal and external dimensions the writers explore with equal fervor:

> "You know, you can talk to a plane. Like a woman. I mean that. And I couldn't talk to a Thunderbolt. But this P 51 now. . . . His eyes go a trifle soft. Has he got a girl waiting somewhere? Every man has a girl waiting somewhere. But right now that girl is second to Megura's Mustang. He can talk to that plane. And maybe the record shows it answers back to him (p. 120).

The legacy of this style of writing reaches down to the present in the way that the air war is recalled. In helping Hub Zemke write *Zemke's Wolf Pack* (1988), Eighth Air Force historian Roger A. Freeman recalls how his own childhood reading of "a paperback called *Fighters Up*" helped him understand what was happening across the fields at Boxsted aerodrome where his father cut grass and Zemke's Fifty-sixth Fighter Group made history. This becomes a history that Freeman finds to be best understood in terms of the exuberant rivalries and lust for high scores that typify this particular phase of the air war. Thus is formed the continuity among contemporaneous and present-day descriptions.

The pilots themselves recall events much as they are dramatized in *Fighters Up*. Metaphors from American high school sports, especially football, characterize Friedheim and Taylor's reporting, together with images from the most popular style of combat a nation long used to peacetime might prefer, that of boxing. Nearly fifty years later, these heroes recount their experiences in almost identical terms. When his first two months (and twenty-six missions) go by without a group kill, during which "both the 4th and the 78th were running up toward double figures," Hub Zemke admits that "I couldn't escape the feeling that I was the guy against the ropes" (1991, p. 102)—a curious use of the metaphor, given that his opponents were not in fact Lt. Col. Arman Peterson and Maj. Don Blakeslee but the pilots of the German air force. Yet such is the way *Fighters Up* had portrayed it: a bunch of fun-loving and constitutionally peaceful Yanks who could bring themselves to fight only by devising competitions among themselves. And this is the clarifying image that Friedheim and Taylor use when explaining Zemke's task as a group leader, one whose "rigorous combat training program had keyed them like fighters waiting for the bell" (1944, p. 16). As for underlying truth, both books report Zemke's past exploits as an actual prizefighter back home before the war.

Hub Zemke himself can see the humor in such descriptive language, amazed that there are so few security restrictions on combat reports that "an almost daily box score of fighter aces and their victories was published just as if it was some sort of sporting event" (1991, p. 177). At times, in more traditional Battle of Britain fashion, this ledgering takes the shape of combat ratios, comparisons of enemies downed to friendlies lost. Every fighter pilot cites such ratios in his memoirs, and Richard Turner goes so far as to post the ultimate factor on the title page of his book, *Big Friend, Little Friend*:

356th Fighter Squadron
354th Fighter Group
Combat: ETO, Nov. 1943-May 1945
4 Battle Stars, Presidential Citation w/ocl
298 enemy a/c destroyed with loss of 22.

But ratios are just an index, a figure to be cited after the battle; what seems to motivate the battle and pace its narrative are the individual races toward top score among the pilots and the larger competition between notably rival groups.

"It became increasingly frustrating to see Mustang groups get most of the choice pitches" (1991, p. 224), Hub Zemke complains, bringing in another sports metaphor to vivify the contest between his Thunderbolt-equipped Fifty-sixth Fighter Group and the P-51 flying Fourth and 357th. Francis Gabreski reports how the rival group commander responded to this frustration. "Zemke challenged us to reach one hundred victories by Sadie Hawkins Day," the date itself created for popular culture by cartoonist Al Capp of L'il Abner fame; needless to say, "The reporters loved the idea and started watching our progress closely" (1991, p. 121). Chief among those reporters were Friedheim and Taylor, whose *Fighters Up* would find its focus and story line in this tournament stylized in the language of high school athletics and measured in terms of a comic strip. "The rivalry between various fighter groups is intense," they report. "But as a practical result, it makes for better protection of the bombers—the primary purpose of an escort mission—and for more Nazi planes destroyed" (1944, p. 77). The competition also serves a journalistic purpose, letting the authors characterize the air war in a way their readers can understand and rally to, almost as parent-spectators cheering on their children's high school team:

> Way back last summer, Col. Hubert Zemke's Thunderbolt group had destroyed 100 Nazi planes in 86 days. That wasn't bad. Nobody else had touched the mark since.
>
> The Mustang group eyed their record. Here they were on their 83rd day, and with only 92 victories. Could they get eight more Huns in three days? Well, they couldn't by sitting around grousing about it, so they went up and had a try. When they came back to circle the home field, they had a new record in their pocket. Eleven victories that day made their score 103 in 83 days. Stephens had the honor of the 100th kill.
>
> But they knew Zemke, and just to be on the safe side they went up the next day and headed for Oschersleben-Halberstadt to support some B-17's. They made it an even dozen planes this day, for a total of 115 (pp. 77-78).

The effect of such racing is infectious; other pilots admire the score and ask each other "Wonder what we could do up there?" (p. 78). For both journalists and flyers, such rivalries and the language to express them put the war in manageable terms, and from such management arose better achievement.

Individual races make for even more colorful material. In *Fighters Up* the focus for Duane Beeson's pursuit of Don Gentile's leading score is told from the perspective of Beeson's crew chief, Tech. Sgt. Willard Wall. And for a very good reason: Beeson is no longer available to the authors of *Fighters Up*, having been shot down by flak while strafing a German airfield. The chapter ends with Wall in mourning, but the journalists' language leaves it uncertain what bothers the crew chief most. "Anyhow, no Hun pilot got Beeson. No flier was better than Beeson," the sergeant is pictured thinking in his solitary bunk. "Flak got the Boise Bee. No flier can avoid flak. It doesn't matter how good you are, with flak. No Hun was good enough to get Beeson." But is the standard for being "good" a measure just against German flyers? Notice what troubles Sergeant Wall: "The blackboard still has the private scores. Beeson twenty-one, Gentile twenty-two. Beeson is twenty-three now. But Gentile is twenty-seven. That's the breaks. Wall lies there looking up at nothing. A couple of other guys go out and leave him to be alone" (1944, p. 135).

Although there is no evidence that such racing for the lead ever became counterproductive, there are many firsthand accounts of how "going for one more kill" was self-consuming. Both Hub Zemke and Francis Gabreski ended the war in German prison camps with orders home in their pockets; neither could resist flying one extra mission before heading back to the United States, and in each case what should have been a crowning victory sealed their operational defeat. On 20 July 1944, early on the very day he's scheduled to leave Boxsted for the United States, Gabreski looks over the operations officer's shoulder to see what's scheduled and is tempted by the prospects. "Schilling was right," Gabreski agrees, "this was the sort of mission that might give a guy the chance to score a kill or two" (1991, p. 170). Crossing the Rhine, he spots an airfield with several Heinkel 111s ripe for picking, so tempting that he decides to "buck the rules" (p. 173) and make a second pass. Is the alerted flak too great a risk? No, it has been pretty light the first time around. And what about violating group orders? "This was my last mission." Gabreski chuckles. "What was Zemke going to do about it? Send me home?" (p. 174).

Neither flak or the CO get him, but his own eagerness does: sweeping too low, he chews up his propellor and bellies in just beyond the field.

Zemke's motivation is more complex. After 154 missions his bags are packed as well, but not for home; he's scheduled to become chief of staff of the Sixty-fifth Fighter Wing, which means a desk job in London. Resisting it to the last minute, he postpones his hour of departure for an escort mission over north-central Germany; a good weather forecast and promise of Luftwaffe action are as tempting to him as they were to Gabreski. "One last show," Zemke fancies. "I would lead A group with the 434th Squadron up front" (1991, p. 245). Also like Gabreski, a flying accident does him in; cloaked in an unanticipated heavy mist east of Hanover, Zemke's Mustang collides with another. Even as he parachutes to captivity he relishes his victory with "a fleeting thought of those bags packed at Wattisham and the desk job at Wing. I didn't intend it this way, but I'd fooled 'em!" (pp. 246-47).

The flyer most aware of this self-consuming drive is John Godfrey. Zemke and Gabreski can joke about the fate their ambitions brought them; reminiscing in retirement, well over four decades after the events, they have the perspective of long, successful lives in which a bit of youthful wildness finds easy excuse. Not so for the man who drafts *The Look of Eagles*, writing in 1957-58 with the knowledge that terminal illness gives him less than a year to live. Moreover, his had been one of the more noteworthy ace races, highlighted by the news media as he and his leader Don Gentile partnered their way to victories over the Luftwaffe while their own scores remained just a hair's breadth apart.

Godfrey, one must recall, has been the classic fighter-jock discipline case, resisting authority and earning himself not punishment but reward. For matters such as going AWOL and keeping an unauthorized pet, the trouble is innocent enough. But when it comes to tactics, his behavior soon makes a mockery of such Air Force ideals as discipline and teamwork. From the beginning Godfrey's motives had been complex, joining the RCAF to avoid the boredom of a dead-end job but, once trained and flying, naming his plane after a brother lost with a torpedoed convoy and eager to even the score. Time and again, he thwarts group policy in favor of personal kills. And once those kills start adding up into a newsworthy competition, the race itself takes prominence.

Finally, to cool things off, the powers that be decide to take the illustrious pair out of action for awhile, sending them back to the States for a morale-building tour. This makes Godfrey no happier than Zemke or Gabreski when their combat days were suspended. But with the perspective of approaching death Godfrey can judge his own culpability in a most remarkable confession:

> The old saying of "Ours is not to reason why" kept buzzing through my head. Evidently the Air Force didn't want Don to return alone as a hero—bad for the morale of the Air Force, probably, which continually stressed teamwork in all of its branches. If Don and I returned together, it would stress the fact that it was as a team that we had achieved success.
>
> The Air Force was right, of course, but the teamwork had become only a means to a personal end. In the race of honors, I—and no doubt Don—had forgotten the sole purpose of war. The "Reggie's Reply" written on my plane had become a mockery of my former purpose. So much had happened since I made that pledge to myself. Now it was no longer revenge I was seeking, nor was I fighting for the way of life which millions of Americans were struggling to protect. My battle was for my own personal glory. My one ambition was to be the top fighter pilot of the war. Where or how I lost my ideals I cannot say. Maybe it was the atmosphere of Debden, with its photographers and newsmen continually searching for heroes (1958, p. 124).

In light of Godfrey's admission, the promotionalism of the day's journalism seems frivolous if not misguided. At the very least, it was a noble effort gone slightly bad, this attempt to make John Godfrey and Don Gentile something more sporting and heroic (and cooperative) than they were or even, in the best of worlds, could be. Take the account in *Fighters Up* from 7 April 1944, when "Today they are taking pictures of Capt. Don Salvadore Gentile, who has destroyed twenty-seven enemy planes" (1944, p. 106). As the script would call for it, the journalists combine Air Force PR lines with the usual sports metaphors, which is where John Godfrey comes in. "And Godfrey, the wing man," they report. "He's the other half of the Gentile-Godfrey brother act. The touchdown Twins. The one-two punch" (p. 110). That Godfrey has by this time forgotten his own brother is a deeper story that must wait fourteen years; for now the message is "Mike and Ike, they look alike. The brother act is sworn in enemy blood" (p. 113). Even the no-longer apt nickname of Godfrey's Mustang, "Reggie's Reply," serves image-making purpose, as the authors remark "It's fitting that a man out for vengeance because of his brother's death should do a brother act" (p. 114). What Friedheim and Taylor can't see, of course, they can't report. But something they do witness is taken firmly off the record: how for the admiring journalists and winding newsreel cameras Gentile is asked to do some stunts and in the process wrecks his plane.

Eagerness for one more score made POWs out of Zemke and Gabreski when they should have been safely finished with action. It is an even greater irony that puts John Godfrey in the Dulag Luft. A habitual scoffer at the ideal of teamwork, he finds himself the victim of an overeager squadron mate whose own violation of this principle sends Godfrey down in a hail of misdirected fire—a common enough occurrence that Marvin Bledsoe can report barely escaping a similar fate in *Thunderbolt* (1982, p. 185). In each case, a wingman so intent on scoring a kill hasn't noticed his bullets hitting his leader. Yet even prison camp can't dampen Godfrey's competitive spirit; seeking better conditions, he goes AWOL from forced marches and cuts his own sweet deals with guards and civilian families. And on repatriation, his first question is about the gun film picturing his last victory, his first act the registering of this kill in his total score.

These latter actions are not reported as confession or apology. Even in the face of a much greater battle, the virtually hopeless fight for his life against Lou Gehrig's disease, Godfrey sees nothing embarrassing about such devotion to scorekeeping. Nor do the authors of *Fighters Up*, who tell a similar (if not riskier) story of Lt. Ralph K. Hofer, a Fourth Fighter Group member pledged to catching the Fifty-sixth. On a March afternoon in 1944 he downs two Me-109s, but when attacking another suffers a runaway propellor. Reason dictates a quick bailout; prudence suggests trying to stretch his flight to neutral Switzerland. But with "Blakeslee's firing burning inside him," he thinks of something else: the gun-camera film locked in his Mustang's left wing. "The two ME 109's he got to-day would bring his total to five," he reflects. "It would cut Zemke's lead by two planes." But not without proof:

> "I wanted to save that film," the lad from Missouri says, grinning. He's tall and slim, boyish looking, embarrassed at talking about himself. So what he did subsequently, in his desperate plight, was to save his film—if you want to put it that way. A former Golden Gloves boxing champion, courage is second nature to him (1944, p. 105).

With "that kind of spirit" Hofer turns his plane from safe haven in Switzerland limps back, across the Alps no less, to save the record of his victories and confirmation of the Fourth's gain on Zemke's Fifty-sixth.

Much has been made of the Blakeslee-Zemke rivalry. Simple givens shape the situation into a natural set of contrasts: Mustangs versus Thunderbolts, veterans versus newcomers, the oldest group (with its Eagle squadron heritage) versus the newest, and so forth.

Strategies were different as well, Blakeslee preaching that his pilots must never be the first to break away in a head-on attack (lest word of such timidity spread among the Luftwaffe), Zemke developing the teamwork idea into a concept writ large as "The Wolf Pack." Even the two leaders' personal situations were different: Blakeslee the tall, handsome, almost movie-starish WASP, Zemke the crusty, ethnic former prizefighter. But starting with these factors, writers like Friedheim and Taylor really poured it on. "The unnecessary pressure imposed by a continual stream of press people to our base whose attitudes were often akin to a sports reporter's" was something Zemke says "we could do without" (1991, p. 178). Consider the colorful language jumping off almost every page of *Fighters Up*. Blakeslee's Mustangs have red-painted noses, "significant" because "in the past five weeks his group tasted blood and went wild" (p. 95). Why so? Because of their record's pursuit by the Fifty-sixth Fighter Group, in which "Zemke's boys began gnawing into the proud lead like rats into cheese." "Rats?" one asks, only to read the journalists' characterization of the rival group's new leader, Don Blakeslee, who is seen as "a strong man with the hint of a Viking about him. A determined face with a strong jaw. Wavy blond hair." At least according to the authors of *Fighters Up* his first orders are not directed with regard to the enemy but rather to "catch Zemke" (p. 99).

Journalists make no apologies for such flamboyance. Rather, they try to justify it. "There is a husky rivalry between fighter plane groups. The duty of the fighter plane is to protect the bombers. What better protection than knocking the Luftwaffe out of the skies?" (pp. 97-99), an assumption bomber tacticians would and did question. But Friedheim and Taylor argue tactics of their own—tactics of personality. "The once-proud ex-Eagles were in a sorry state, compared to Zemke's group," they report. "Blakeslee put his chemist's mind to work breaking the situation down into its missing component parts" (p. 100). His pilots, he feels, are missing chances because they lack sufficient motivation to find them. Hence "this blond Viking of the skies" (p. 102) concocts the rivalry in order to catalyze the action he wants: "Group spirit. Morale. A certain reckless camaraderie. The chemist planned for a spark, and he got a wildfire" (p. 104). And he also produced pilots like John Godfrey, who thirteen years later would wonder where his idealism had disappeared.

Hub Zemke laments that the journalists covering his group responded like sports reporters, but over at the Fourth Don Blakeslee seems to have played right into their hands. "Combat flying is the greatest sport in the world," he says on the record for *Fighters Up*. "There is no more exciting game. The stakes are supreme; they're not money, but human lives. You bet your life against that Hun coming head-on toward you with his guns blinking" (1944, p. 102).

Were there risks in taking such attitudes and acting on them? James Howard, commanding the 354th Fighter Group, takes time in *Roar of the Tiger* to do some ledgering and comes up with some interesting figures—not just total victories (the number *Fighters Up* and some individual memoirists make so much of), but ratios that consider the number of planes lost as well. Here Hub Zemke's group is seen as losing 128 pilots, a ratio of 1:8. Blakeslee's group has 241 pilots lost, not just 113 more but a loss-to-kill ratio of 1:4, an absolutely terrible rate of attrition. Howard's own group lost just 78, for an admirable 1:12 ratio.

"These groups all operated in the same theater, facing the same enemy fighters and flak," Howard reasons. "There shouldn't have been such a disparity of losses to victories unless the pilots felt they had been encouraged rashly to do or die. Impressionable young pilots, aiming for glory, should have been disciplined to follow the basic principles of survival." But how is this possible when a leader barks "Get Zemke!" and encourages his men to pace themselves in a world that sees their Fifty-sixth Group colleagues as tearing into cheese like rats and themselves as sportsmen wagering their lives. "It seems that some fighter groups, the Fourth Group especially, fostered or failed to restrain a reckless attitude among its pilots. It was all right to be courageous as long as you were not reckless," Howard concludes. "There is a big difference. In the words of George Patton, 'Let the other SOB die for his country, not you'" (1991, pp. 273-74).

"I've often wondered which scared us the most on that first mission," Richard Turner writes in *Big Friend, Little Friend*, "meeting the Germans or displeasing Colonel Blakeslee" (1969, p. 21). When a new pilot asks at briefing what happens if a German pilot approaching him head-on is under the same orders as Blakeslee has given (never to break away), the CO is described by James Howard as looking down at the young man with a contemptuous smile and saying "In that case you've earned your flight pay the hard way!" (1991, p. 198). Later on in *The Roar of the Tiger* Howard reports just such an incident when Col. Ken Martin collides with a German pilot equally unwilling to swerve aside. Miraculously, both survive, although gravely injured. After his return from POW camp, Martin relates that "his last thought was not of his family, but of Blakeslee's caustic words, 'Never break for a Kraut'" (p. 240).

Yet despite all these excesses, the American fighter pilots flying from England were outstandingly successful. Every memoirist from this command takes time to ponder what made the type so successful. Some, like L.C. Beck, Jr., devote the better part of their narrative to such discernment. Beck's title, *Fighter Pilot*, codifies his idea. "A 'Fighter Pilot' is, I believe, somewhat like a highly trained person in any profession—an artist—you might say. It is quite common to hear of a very talented movie star 'blowing up' and completely losing control of his temper," the young pilot explains. "A state of extreme nervousness exists and if the person is not careful to get the proper rest and relaxation he will very shortly have a 'nervous upset'" (1946, pp. 88-89). This is the flip side to fighter-jock flamboyance: nerves strung to tautness even before combat, trained as fighter pilots are to react quickly while hurtling through all three dimensions at extremely high speed. In *To Fly and Fight* Bud Anderson sees this quality emerging as early as combat training in Nevada, where he and Chuck Yeager are already building reputations for outrageousness, skill, and daring. "A fighter-pilot mentality was taking firm root now," he records. "Living close to the edge sort of went with the job. Daring, audacity, creativity, flair—these things were as much a part of a good fighter pilot's makeup as skill and sound judgment, and were encouraged, within certain parameters. Sometimes, of course, we stretched those a little. The rest of the time, more than a little" (1990, p. 55). Much is made of the pilots with sharp eyes; Chuck Yeager in his Mustang and Robert S. Johnson in his Thunderbolt are the two whose visual capabilities are cited most often, each of them able to pick out tiny specks of German fighters long before the others in their squadrons. So too is aggressiveness—not just the ability to surge off on one mission and come back wrung out yet victorious, but the stamina to continue doing this day after day. Boxing and football again provide metaphors for struggle, especially protracted struggle. But even the most dedicated struggling has its limits, and at the other end of fighter-pilot recklessness are the variations of cutting loose on leave and restoring one's nerves at the rest-and-relaxation "flak houses" set up on idyllic country estates throughout England.

Of all USAAF commands, these boisterous, fun-loving, yet lethally serious fighter pilots were bound together by the most extensive of interlocking structures. At base there was the two-plane element of leader and wingman, then two elements to form a flight and so on upwards to the eighteen-plane squadron and the three-squadron group. Each was important for its own role in tactics. Yet ultimately the fighter pilot, unlike pilots in any other command, was on his own. In the book that did so much to establish the fighter jock as the key person whose heroic business linked victory in World War II to victory over the physical limits of atmosphere, gravity, and ultimately space, William R. Lundgren singles out solitary achievement as the defining attribute. *Across the High Frontier* (1955) finds this quality not just in the work itself but in the nature of the man who does it: Chuck Yeager, who with everything from personal background and the nature of his Air Force commission limiting his chances managed to succeed where even those best equipped were forecast to fail.

Looking at the Bell X-1, designed to break a possibly unbreakable sound barrier, Yeager is quoted as responding to the situation in simple terms: "Whoever flies the plane is going to be entirely on his own" (p. 44). Riding on this test is not only the X-1 and not even just Yeager himself, but rather the type that Yeager is: "the future of common men, of men like Yeager [and his similarly self-made commander] who are born into the world with nothing and who come of age with nothing to recommend them except their personal courage and ability." In 1942-45 and the raw beginnings of the space program the door was still open to such types; as fighter pilots it was these qualities that let them flourish. Selecting Yeager, otherwise undereducated and underranked, is risky, for "When it has finally been done, no one must ever be able to say, You see, this type of fellow is wrong. Let's close the door. The door would thereafter be shut. And who would reopen it?" (p. 51). But with his success, and especially with the style of his success, Chuck Yeager not only keeps the door from being shut on the fighter jocks of World War II but makes them the image of America's postwar spirit:

> You want this project, not just to prove yourself or to measure yourself against the rest, and not for the fame it might bring. You've had a glance at the future, touched the unknown. You've got to go on and see what's there because you can only go on alone. This is the thing, this chance to accomplish something alone, something that's really important, and to do it without depending on any other man. The pilot who flies the X-1 into the sonic range will, in the last analysis, make the decision himself. And when he goes, he'll go alone. This much you know (p. 76).

That fighter jocks were expected to perform together adds an enervating quality to their professional lives. The key, as Richard Turner explains in *Big Friend, Little Friend*, is having "the knack of flying as a team and thinking as one, regardless of who led the flight" (1969, p. 10). He credits his success to the example set by the group commander, James H. Howard, whose mutual support tactics had been developed among one of the greatest discipline challenges in air combat history, the Flying Tigers. Howard's ideal was a simple one, expressed in his own *Roar of the Tiger* by reflecting that "There were no 'hot' pilots in the 354th, only 'excellent' pilots" (1991, p. 274). The difficulties thus presented are considerable: taking the talents and disposition of utmost individuality and having two or more persons so gifted function together.

Those who do best with team spirit see it as an ideal themselves. Not an easy practice, but something at which they will necessarily fail. For Robert S. Johnson, it is the ideal that motivates his flying career and stands enshrined as the first episode described in *Thunderbolt!* Where so many other flyers recall their first flight, usually as a child being thrilled by a barnstormer, this eventual twenty-seven-victory ace remembers not a single airplane but a formation. "There were three of them," his memoir begins. "Each with double wings and a whirling propellor flashing in the bright Oklahoma sun." Not only were the aircraft together, but they seemed glued to each other as they dove from above. "The three pursuits were almost into the ground, when the planes were wrenched from their dives. Three hands, operating as one, gripping control sticks in three different cockpits, flawlessly timed, hauling back." Enthralled, the youngster follows their every motion, "struck dumb, staring, as the pursuits zoomed up and over, twisted and turned intricately as if a single hand were maneuvering them, then floated mysteriously in an invisible balance of their wings and gravity" (1990, p. 1).

This is the perfection Johnson will aim for and not always hit, creating problems for himself and for his leaders. He gets his squadron's first confirmed kill, but not in the correct manner. Spotting an Me-109 below, he peels off. "Unfortunately, he did it so fast that no one could follow him," Frances Gabreski recounts in *Gabby*, "so he made the attack alone." The problem is that Johnson has been flying not in the lead spot but as number four. Yet a victory has been scored. Gabreski's reaction is complex, showing equal measures of anger, admiration, and compromise:

> I couldn't stay mad at Bob, because my policy about air fighting was a little different than that of many squadron commanders. In lots of outfits it was strict policy that the flight and element leaders did the shooting and the wingmen protected their tails. I told my guys that once they were really working as a team, it didn't make any difference who led and who followed. If my wingman called in an enemy aircraft and I couldn't spot it immediately, I'd

tell him to lead the attack. Now I'm the wingman and he's the gunner. Time was the most important element, and the few seconds it might take me to pick up the target could cost us the tactical advantage that made the difference between making the kill and *getting* killed (1991, pp. 102-3).

As group commander, Hub Zemke is no happier, yet he goes through the same complex of emotions as does Gabreski when, despite being reprimanded, the pilot repeats his misbehavior, this time in pursuit of a FW-190:

> When Johnson saw the Focke-Wulfs below us he just peeled over and went down after the leader, got close up behind him and blasted him out of the sky. This was in direct contravention of the rule whereby a wingman always stayed with his element leader unless otherwise directed. It was not the first time that Johnson had been guilty of ignoring the rules and he had to be disciplined. It was difficult to give a man a chewing out for action which resulted in the destruction of an enemy plane. In doing so I doubt I endeared Bob to his group commander. Privately, it was good to know that I had pilots of such aggressive caliber. Also, I was aware of my own failure to call other flights down to attack and realized that in the future flight leaders should be instructed to use their own discretion and go into the attack if the group leader was preoccupied in combat. Without checking individual initiative the team effort had to be fostered to such a degree that every squadron and flight leader automatically followed out battle plans for a given situation. More and more I was coming to realize that if we stood any chance of really beating the Luftwaffe it was going to be through bringing as much of the group's firepower into action on each operation, rather than just picking off one or two enemy planes when the opportunity arose. To this end we had got to increase the emphasis on training. A lot of our people already thought themselves "gung-ho" fighter pilots but they still had an awful lot to learn (1991, pp. 108-9).

Johnson's reaction is the most complex of all. During training he has heartily supported the team concept, acknowledging that being able to fly and fight with others is what "separates the men from the boys" (1990, p. 49). But as the action of *Thunderbolt!* takes him into combat he finds the thrill of engagement taking precedence. "Somehow I had on several occasions ended up alone in our fights with the Germans," he ponders, unable to see how from Gabreski's and Zemke's perspectives he was flying fourth and not first and thus unable to be accompanied—in other words, unable to picture himself as part of a group. "I'd damaged several more enemy fighters, but my flight leader, and Zemke as well, were irritated because of their conviction that I was playing the role of the lone wolf. And it wasn't that at all! The only way to fight was to get in there and *fight*—and before I knew it, I'd be a lone Thunderbolt in the middle of black-crossed planes" (pp. 134-35). Perhaps this is where the men and boys *are* separated, for at this stage of the war Johnson is still thinking in schoolboy terms. Getting ready for a mission, he experiences a "quiver of excitement" that he has felt before, as a student boxer "waiting the eternity of seconds before the bell rings, waiting to shuffle forward, to have my head rocked back by a stinging jab, waiting for the fear to leave me, for the opponent's blow to wash my fear away, until I could rush into him, swinging, alive with the moments of the fight" (pp. 137-38). What the young pilot fails to realize is that his understanding that "the only way to fight was to get in there and *fight*" is based not on air combat tactics but on the isolation of the boxing ring. It will take more training before he realizes that as a P-47 pilot he is not being shoved out there alone.

Yet in the necessary battle between individualism and group spirit, Johnson finds that his sharpest talents work to alienate him. Dutifully in formation, keeping his measured distance in the "Zemke fan," he's dumbstruck that "The Thunderbolts drone on, utterly oblivious of the sixteen fighters streaking in. Am I the only man in the Group who sees these planes?" (p. 141). He resists the temptation to break into them, and as a result his section is hit. The blows rain down upon him like a beleaguered prizefighter in the ring; for a time, he thinks he will have to box his way out of the jammed cockpit. Finally, harassed by a persistent FW-190, Johnson's Thunderbolt is forced to absorb unrelenting punishment like a heavyweight on his last legs. Yet despite all this individualism it is a team effort that saves the pilot, Hub Zemke coming up to fly alongside and talk Johnson into a safe bailout near base.

Having done everything possible by himself, Robert Johnson takes the last step with the aid of a teammate. After this, he is less of a lone wolf and more the member of a wolf pack, seeing offensive strength in numbers and realizing that he is more likely to be picked off when alone. It is in these circumstances that he can glory not in an individual score but as a member of the first squadron to make 100 aerial kills. Yet the progress toward such teamwork has been long and hard.

The workable balance of individual and team is found in squadron life. Here the pilots are incredibly close, simply because so many of them are lost in combat. "Twenty pilots start out together," Chuck Yeager explains to William R. Lundgren in *Across the High Frontier*. "Half of them are killed and the rest of you in the group come closer and closer together" (1955, p. 136). The intimate quality of squadron life is what pleases Yeager in that other most individual of accomplishments, test piloting advanced aircraft well past limits never reached by others. Danger and attrition are factors, but even more so is the brotherhood of such work; only a very few can do it, and these few are here together, insulated from the rest. On descent from altitude after transsonic testing Yeager and his buddy in the chase plane dogfight in playful mock combat; but at other times serious arguments in the test section are settled with such contests, and motivating everything is the goal to be number one—the highest and the fastest, and therefore the best. Exclusivity was long the hallmark of fighter jocks; being at "top of the pyramid" now distinguished top test pilots from all others. And the best test pilots—those able to do things the company flyers couldn't, such as fly formation and wrestle their planes through violent maneuvers—were veterans of the fighter clan.

Among RAF pilots in Fighter Command, this clannishness had extended to their adversaries in the Luftwaffe, at least when having the upper hand and able to respond as gentlemen. Such fabled sporting behavior was more common earlier in the war, before destruction had reached almost apocalyptic dimensions. Historically, a reader of memoirs finds it expressed most in the accounts of either university-trained, auxiliary squadron flyers (members of what in prewar years had been called the world's finest flying clubs) or of the successful, noteworthy, famous, and therefore most confident pilots. Examples are declining to kill a disabled opponent; breaking off combat after the other's ammunition has been exhausted; and hosting a captured German flyer at mess, serving an elaborate meal, and exchanging toasts before the more serious formalities of confinement begin.

The American pilots, especially the more flamboyant fighter jocks, did not always share this attitude. Instead, the usual approach was more businesslike and eminently pragmatic. In the process of scoring his twenty-third victory, Robert S. Johnson pauses to admire his adversary's skill, particularly when the pilot makes a turn tighter and quicker than Johnson has ever seen. "That man was *good!*" he exclaims in *Thunderbolt!*, surprised that after such a brilliant escape maneuver the German brings his FW-190 around for a head-on attack. But when the enemy finally breaks away, Johnson's admiration becomes the motivating factor in his pursuit. "I didn't want this boy to reach home," he claims. "The canopy leaped into the air as the pilot jerked the release; I pulled around tight to get my bullets into him before he could get out of the airplane." Were this 1940 and the adversaries Bader and Galland, here might be the time to stop firing, as in terms of a fighters' duel the contest is over. But instead the American continues, describing something unlikely to be encountered in any Battle of Britain narrative from either side. "He had one leg outside the cockpit when the slugs smashed him back inside," Johnson describes, then explains why he's taken the kill to this extreme. "That's one man who would never sight again on our planes; if I hadn't gotten him, then he certainly would have shot down several of our fighters or bombers. He was as good as I'd ever met" (1990, p. 236). The very qualities that might have saved a Luftwaffe ace with a gentleman in the Duke of Hamilton's City of Glasgow Squadron here consign him to death at the hands of an American who has bested him. Such is the deadly pragmatism of the war now being fought.

Johnson also shares another typical attitude, that of evening the score. Thoughts like these are expressed earlier in his combat career, especially in the joy of his first victory. "I'd made a vow that I would try to flame a Jerry for every one of my close friends shot down over Europe," he admits. "And I fully intended to do just that" (p. 133). It's an attitude shared by his squadron as led by Francis Gabreski, proclaimed in their nickname, "The Avengers." When a friend is shot down before him, Johnson's reaction is elemental: "I wanted that German. I wanted to kill him. I've never before been so badly afflicted with the urge to kill as I was that moment" (p. 204), words more likely to come from a Jimmy Cagney gangster movie than from the Arthurian lore mythologized as the way of the early RAF. Throughout his story Johnson is never seen giving quarter or letting either sympathy or admiration for a foe hold him back, not even when he experiences it at the hands of a Focke-Wulf pilot who after failing to bring the disabled but still sturdy Thunderbolt down "shakes his head in wonder," salutes, and with a rocking of wings pulls away to let Johnson limp home safely (p. 156).

On the other hand Americans are neophytes to battle. Many pilots enter combat without appreciating what's at risk, and in their first firefights have to wake up to an enemy's threat with the stark realization that "He's trying to kill me"; such is the split-second passage from innocence to experience that characterizes an early scene in Bill Price's *Close Calls* (1992, p. 37). Looking back on his career in *To Fly and Fight*, Bud Anderson emphasizes how casual this sense of being experienced can be. For all the engagements he fought alongside Chuck Yeager and others, only once was he nearly shot down.

But is he interested in having a historian look up the name of this adversary who nearly did him in? "I never saw any point," Anderson scoffs. "He was someone who was trying to kill me, is all" (1990, p. 6). Yet records of such combats do exist, and postwar friendships have resulted from a flyer's belief that his adversary has shown mercy. Merle Olmsted tells just such a story in *The 357th Over Europe* (1994), of how Lt. Hollis "Bud" Nowlin shot down Hauptmann Gunther Schack on an escort mission over East Prussia. With his Messerschmitt's coolant system hit, Schack bellies in, with Nowlin's Mustang not firing on his tail or strafing but flying at his side, then waving and breaking away:

> In the late 1980s historian Bill Graham brought the two together again when Bud Nowlin and his wife paid a visit to Schack at his home in Germany. In the fall of 1991, Gunther Schack was an honored guest of the Nowlins and the 357th Fighter Group at their fall reunion in Georgia.
>
> For over four decades, Schack had wondered why the P-51 pilot had not finished him off. After meeting Bud Nowlin, he has now come to the conclusion that Nowlin was a good man who did not desire to kill a crippled fellow airman (p. 80).

Significantly, neither Nowlin or Olmsted (who worked on the ground crew) let this stand as an answer. There were other factors at work, both Americans admit, such as the facts that Nowlin was alone, running low on fuel, and out of sight from his group.

Thou shalt not kill. The lesson remains in nearly every pilot's memory as the least ambiguous of commandments, and even the unsentimental Bud Anderson finds that it still has binding force. He resolves the problem of being a fighter pilot by recalling Bible verses condoning the smiting of enemies. "But I never strafed anyone out in the open, unarmed," he counsels. "I strafed airplanes, of course. A tank, a column of trucks, locomotives, gun emplacements. But rightly or wrongly I stopped short of strafing people just standing there, civilian or not. Everyone draws his own moral line. That was mine. I never strafed parachutes, either" (1990, p. 111). In *George Preddy, Top Mustang Ace* (1991), Joe Noah emphasizes how his cousin never took shots at a caboose; that was where the trainmen rode, and Preddy's father was a freight conductor (p. 105). When Americans do mention shooting at Germans in parachutes, it's almost always within two explicit circumstances: when he has seen the Luftwaffe pilot doing it himself just before his own bailout, or when a falling airman is seen engulfed in fire. "Had I been in that dreadful situation I would have wanted the same deliverance" (p. 211), says Hub Zemke, after putting a dying Focke-Wulf pilot out of his misery.

"You've got to always respect your enemy," Francis Gabreski describes himself telling the pilots under his command. "The Germans have been at war for quite a while, and they have a lot of experience. So whatever encounter you may get into, always remember you have to respect their ability to shoot you down" (1991, p. 71). It is this type of respect that prompts American pilots to stop short of brutalizing their adversaries. Instead, there seems a mutual recognition that each is in the same business, and that the business is not killing the other but taking down the other's machine. As with the Eagles' first encounters, the target remains the plane, with occasional surprise that there is in fact a man in it. "Usually when I shot down a plane, I secretly hoped the pilot would be able to bail out," Richard Turner admits, adding that the one time he feels "a real desire to kill an enemy pilot" is when he observes a Me-109 taking cruel advantage of an already grievously disabled B-17 (1969, p. 43). Instead, the more common reaction is that of Marvin Bledsoe in *Thunderbolt*, who feels terrible when seeing a German pilot trapped in the cockpit of his burning Me-109. On a sortie just two hours earlier, Bledsoe has had the kind of face-to-face contact that personalizes war, just as a colleague has scored his first victory: "I was sure the pilot had been killed, but suddenly a parachute appeared. He had bailed out before his ship exploded. I flew close by him and could see the terrified look on his face. He was obviously afraid I would shoot him. He was startled when I gave him a wave. He grinned weakly and waved back. It was a strange world" (1982, p. 128).

When Turner downs a Messerschmitt and its pilot hits the silk, reactions on both sides are even more dramatic. Because his initial burst of fire has flown wide but scared the German into abandoning his plane, Turner speculates that it might be well to have film of the flyer in his parachute as proof of victory. He flips the gun switch to "camera only," but pauses when "the thought crossed my mind that this circuit had been known to foul up and fire the guns, so, I restrained my desire to get the confirming picture of my victim." Swinging past, he sees his adversary pulling his arms up to his face, expecting to be shot. When Turner gives a waggle of the wings instead, the German starts "waving his arms and grinning like a Cheshire cat" (1969, p. 61). The American celebrates his tenth victory with an act of sympathy but also a dose of pragmatism, hoping that word would spread among the Luftwaffe about such decent behavior and encourage them to follow suit.

There are, closer to the war's end, even more intimate encounters. During his lengthy interrogation before being interned as a prisoner of war, Frances Gabreski is treated to social occasions by his Luftwaffe captors: the customary pilots' banquet, of course, but also a visit to a public swimming pool in Frankfurt:

> There were all kinds of people there—girls, mothers and fathers, and so forth. But what impressed me were all the young guys with arms and legs missing who were there, former soldiers who had been grievously wounded in battle. That had a real impact on me.
>
> This was a reality of war that I had been shielded from until now. War in the cockpit of a fighter was impersonal. We weren't shooting at people. We were shooting at machines, destroying machines. We saw the pieces flying off an airplane. We didn't see the end of it, the bloodshed. I was a little bit shook by the swimming pool visit (1991, p. 190).

Yet even machines and facilities, when viewed up close and out of combat, have their effect. Richard Turner notes it as German airfields are occupied, now devastated but only recently bustling with activity much like he himself knows. "I felt a twinge of compassion for the pilots who must have watched the destruction of their irreplaceable fighting planes," he notes. "Pilots come as close as anyone can to love and affection for an inanimate machine." In this and most other things the Luftwaffe flyers, he can now see, were "not much different from ourselves" (1969, pp. 143-44). Concluding *Roar of the Tiger*, James Howard tries to resist such sentiments, especially when the German surrender brings crowds of former enemies to admire his Mustang and propose a feast "for the conquering heroes." This, to Howard, brings no pleasure. "At that moment, I had a kind of sinking sensation that here we were suddenly friendly with an enemy we had been fighting for two years" (1991, p. 291). Yet the combative spirit lives on, even in peace. for fighter pilots must be fighter pilots—or, more accurately, fighter jocks. Among the surrendering Germans is a Messerschmitt pilot who insists his Me-109 can outdogfight any P-51. To settle it, the German and one of Howard's squadron mates take off in their respective planes and go through their paces above the field, much as Chuck Yeager and his cohort of test pilots were to resolve arguments in coming years.

There is a thrill to such interaction that eclipses even what Don Blakeslee savored as the ultimate sporting event where life or death figured as the wager. Some of the finest descriptions in fighter pilot memoirs involve no fighting at all, but rather just the beauty of these forces being engaged. On patrol above the Frisian Islands during the winter of 1943-44, Bill Price recalls, "We were at high altitude on a brilliant, sunny day but below was a complete undercast of white, creamy cloud layer." Although *Close Calls* has plenty combat sequences, this will not be one of them. Instead the author describes the aesthetics of this moment: "Suddenly a lone ME-109 appeared just above the cloud. It was a beautifully painted aircraft—red and gray colors with Maltese Crosses and Swastikas" (1992, pp. 39-40). The Messerschmitt does not engage Price's flight, but just sits out there, to observe and be observed. Perhaps the German pilot was remarking the same lovely colors decorating the checkerboard-trimmed P-47s.

Even combat action itself brings out uncommonly fine descriptions. Consider how in *To Fly and Fight* Bud Anderson animates the situation of flying escort well back in the bomber stream while its leading elements are being attacked: "Through our headsets we could hear the war, working its way back toward us, coming straight at us at hundreds of miles per hour" (1990, p. 3). When he does go after a German fighter, language is stretched to convey how things look and feel. "I hose the Messerschmitt down the way you hose down a campfire," Anderson writes, "methodically, from one end to another, not wanting to make a mistake here. The 109 shakes like a retriever coming out of the water, throwing off pieces. He slows, almost stops, as if parked in the sky, his propellor just windmilling, and he begins smoking heavily" (pp. 8-9). Sometimes the memoirist's search for metaphors sounds a comic note, as when Lt. Raymond Littge, quoted in *George Preddy, Top Mustang Ace*, describes his pursuit of an Me-262: "There was nothing funny about these jet jobs, but this one was having trouble with his landing gear. It kept dropping down and reminded me of a kid who was running away from someone, and whose pants kept dropping down" (Noah and Sox 1991, p. 128). Other times comparisons from the world of childhood are tragic, as when Bud Anderson details the death throes of an out-of-control B-17, alternately stalling and swooping "like some child's balsa glider" (1990, p. 88).

Then there are the scenes that animate themselves. It happens to the bomber stream that Marvin Bledsoe sees flying through the target barrage. They enter it in perfect order, then are obscured by heavy black smoke. "By the time they came out on the other wide," Bledsoe notes, "their formation had been ripped apart. Planes were staggering all over the sky from the impact of the flak. I saw two bombers explode and disappear without a trace. A flash, a puff of smoke, then nothing but blue sky" (1982, p. 211). For Capt. Glendon Davis, quoted in *The 357th Over Europe*, the fate of a crashing FW-190 is seen in quicker transition: "After about two more turns, he stalled and he was firing his right wing guns as he crashed through the small grove of trees, becoming completely obscured by them. He emerged on the other side, a flaming ball of wreckage" (Olmsted 1994, p. 41).

Sometimes the comparisons are funny, as when in his autobiography, *Yeager* (1985) Chuck Yeager has to laugh at his own futile pursuit of two Me-262 jets: "Chasing those guys, I was a fat man running uphill to catch a trolley" (p. 60). But everyday life offers fearful correspondences as well. "On the first sighting of a German plane," John Godfrey confides in *The Look of Eagles*, "I always got the same sensation a person would feel if his speeding car hit a slippery surface and slid out of control" (1958, p. 114). Yet in flight a pilot can become quite the lyricist about this earth he has just left. Training at night, Robert Johnson admires the lights below, especially when they come alive with "the caterpillar glow of a passenger train gliding across the black, preceded by a tiny shower of sparks and tinted orange flame from the locomotive or the firefly gleam of a lonely automobile in the midst of darkened earth slowly piercing the silver gloom" (1990, p. 73). Even on combat missions as a seasoned veteran, he can grace the latter pages of *Thunderbolt!* with virtual rhapsodies of transcending the clouds only to create his own, "a cottony swath of vapor in the heavens, streaming majestically behind each fighter almost as if the killer airplanes sought in vain to flee from the pursuing condensation" (p. 239). Even destructive power can be deftly described, as when the stream of 1,200 heavy bombers is attacked and opens fire. "One moment the sky was filled with only black shapes of airplanes," Johnson notes; "the next instant all hell broke loose. The heavens came alive with countless motes of light, searing bursts of fire, flame dancing and sparkling" (p. 216). As the German fighters do their work, things turn ugly. "It was a picture that only the devil could have enjoyed," as John Godfrey puts it. Yet even he feels compelled to paint it in language as best he can. "Planes were rent by fiery explosions; white blossoms of parachutes could be seen here and there as the victims of the air battle drifted to earth" (1958, p. 106).

The fighter pilot of World War II may well see himself as a solitary artist. When tactics demand it, he can function as a team; quite often he will have to follow as a wingman, sticking to his leader like glue, almost as if he doesn't exist as a separate entity. But when it comes to contemplating the war and describing his own part in it, his unique position as an observer comes into artistic play. He, after all, is the only one all alone, above it all in his single-place cockpit, able to dive in or zoom out of the action almost at will. His only real enemies are the German pilots as solitary and empowered as himself.

Although USAAF politics tried to paint strategic bombing as the war's truly victorious force, it is the fighter jocks in their Thunderbolts and Mustangs who emerge as the perceived heroes of America's air war fought from England. Heroism identifies with an individual; you can't fit a sixty-mile-long bomber stream or even a ten-man crew on the front of a Wheaties box. Teamwork was the party line for commanders, but it seemed in the nature of the fighter pilot's role to contradict it whenever possible. Reckless flamboyance fueled the hunter's most important attribute, his aggressive willingness for a fight at any time; sighting an enemy, his instantaneous reaction had to be to attack rather than flee or even pause to reason out the circumstance. The chip remained forever on his shoulder, the challenge to his enemies always to knock it off. To *try* to knock it off, that is. No real fighter pilot could ever think for a moment that it might be done.

Against all the strange new postwar forces the fighter jock sailed on as individualism's best promise. Atomic deterrence, cold war politics, even a sense of military and industrial organization so complex as to suggest a new order ruled by engineers and sociologists; all this could be stood down by the solitary gunman in his P-51, F-86, X-1 rocket plane or whatever the scientists would next devise. Facing the sound barrier, Chuck Yeager succeeded as only one man can do alone, the fine point of a pyramid that no matter how broadly based with hundreds of designers and scores of supporting crew still came down to the ultimate efforts of the pilot out there alone.

How then is the story told? In his autobiography Yeager sees the problem. "You can't watch yourself fly," he admits. "But you know when you're in sync with the machine. . . . You can make that airplane talk, and like a good horse, the machine knows when it's in competent hands." But you can only do it alone, knowing what you can risk and aware that you can only be wrong once. It is just that solitary responsibility that excuses what in other circumstances would be the most horrible egotism. Above all, Yeager counsels, you must be honest to yourself, even when that honesty is unattractive:

> You smile reading newspaper stories about a pilot in a disabled plane that maneuvered to miss a schoolyard before he hit the

ground. That's crap. In an emergency situation, a pilot only thinks about one thing—survival. You battle to survive right down to the ground: you think about nothing else. Your concentration is riveted on what to try next. You don't say anything on the radio, and you aren't even aware that a schoolyard exists. That's exactly how it is (1985, p. 119).

Chapter 3

Bombers

BOMBERS MAKE FREQUENT appearances in fighter pilot stories, but almost always as planes going down. It is never a pretty sight, but the observer still feels compelled to note what happens, such as when a direct hit from flak takes out a B-17 over Rennes. In *Thunderbolt!*, Robert S. Johnson tells how "In an instant smoke obscured the airplane; a ripping blast hurled it backward from the formation. Then came the dark shapes of men leaping into space, and the joyful sight of silk opening, of ten men dropping safely." The plane itself dies a slow death, slowly falling off to plunge earthward "like a flaming meteor" (1990, p. 188). It is a scene that happens again and again, often fifty times for each thousand-plane raid. Attrition among the bomber forces was the worst for any arm of service in the war.

From the bombers' point of view, the most characteristic narrative becomes that of the victim. This is an irony, of course, coming from a command whose function was the most offense-inclined of the war, dropping high explosives directly on the enemy homeland, military and civilian alike. Yet this is the tone familiar in so many bomber memoirs, from contemporaneous accounts through the reminiscences of half a century later.

Consider *Skyways to Berlin* (1943), the product of two USAAF public relations officers, Maj. John M. Redding and Capt. Harold Leyshon. As a tool for homefront morale, the book's title promises to bring the war to the enemy's capital. Its cover projects B-17s in formation over Berlin, but only as a photo collage. It would be another year before an actual USAAF attack on Berlin, on 4 March 1944. There were short-range raids beforehand, but Redding and Leyshon describe them in an oddly passive way: not in terms of devastation visited upon enemy installations, but rather with a focus on the suffering and sacrifice undergone by American crews.

The first person introduced in *Skyways to Berlin* is the chaplain, the first story told is his narrative of rushing out to administer last rites to a mortally wounded bombardier, with the dying man's kid brother—also a bombardier—at his side. It is no surprise that by chapter's end the kid brother is lost as well, "killed in action over his Norden bombsight" (p. 24). Not just a crewmember but a brother is lost; then the aggrieved himself is killed, all told from the chaplain's point of view. But in selecting the story of bombardiers as first casualties, the authors immediately reverse the path of aggression: not from a bombsight down, but from the enemy's land upwards.

Throughout Redding and Leyshon's volume crewmen are forever dragging their buddies from guns they've kept firing while breathing their last, seizing the grips with ungloved hands to ward off marauding Focke-Wulfs and Messerschmitts in the subzero wind. Disabled Fortresses turn back to offer cover for more seriously shot-up planes; the top gunner in a ditched B-17 keeps firing at the German fighters who would strafe his escaping crewmates, firing even as water engulfs his position and the plane sinks. With a wealth of material to draw upon, the authors can arrange their story any way they wish. And at least one is a literary artist at heart, for later on in Dale Smith's *Screaming Eagle* (1990) Redding is encountered not at any bomb group's base but in London, working on a novel about the Eighth Air Force.

Yet even within the war bomber crews can write with the sensitivity of novelists, and the nature of their narratives suggests that *Skyways to Berlin* may not have been far off target. The earliest bomber memoir remains one of the very best: Bert Stiles's *Serenade to the Big Bird* (1947). His role as victim, albeit a heroic victim, is confirmed by circumstance. As copilot, his part is not a happy one, never able to please his pilot. And so he wishes for a plane of his own—not another B-17 to captain, for his crew life has not been that happy, either, but rather a P-51 Mustang, which he wishes on like the moon:

> Every time when there was a new moon, a slim silver curve of a moon low in the sky, the P-51s would be up there playing around in the moonlight.

You can wish on new moons, but a gipsy dame in New York once told me never to wish for myself on a new moon, because it would never come true, and might even boomerang and come true just the opposite.

So I'd watch the 51s and think about wishing for one, and de cided the gipsy dame might be right, and there would be no sense in throwing a wrench in the works when I wanted one so bad. So I'd wish the rainbows would be hitting in the Colorado River, or wish the babies in London all got enough milk tomorrow, or the dames in Orange, New Jersey, all got enough loving, and let it go at that (p. 61).

Here is where readers share Stiles's victimhood, for on the first page of his book's text, before crewing and first mission and everything else, is a "Note on the Author" that summarizes Bert Stiles's past and lack of a future: "Instead of returning to America" after his tour of thirty-five bomber missions was complete, "he requested to be transferred to fighters. On 26th November 1944 he was shot down in a P-51 on an escort mission to Hanover. He died at the age of 23" (p. 6). And so not even in the illusory freedom of the fighters, sporting with the moon itself, is there salvation from the bomber's fate. In creating over 900,000 enemy casualties, their hopes become casualties themselves.

Most memoirists survive, of course, and tell their stories from the comforting distance of middle or advancing age. Yet here too is the impulse to write like a literary artist—or rather to cast things as a master cinematographer. Both top gunner/flight engineer John Comer and bombardier Fred Koger begin their stories long after the war, back on visits to their old airbases in England. In *Combat Crew* (1988), it's 1972 when Comer walks the site of Ridgewell Airdrome, yet "All at once I was transported back three decades in time," hearing engines revving up for takeoff, smelling the mix of oil and gasoline, and feeling the vibrations of his mighty B-17 as it struggles to clear the runway with a full load of bombs and fuel (p. 11). *Countdown!* (1990) has Koger leaning against the control tower at Poddington, "a sixty-year-old man . . . coming thousands of miles to wallow in nostalgia" as he tries "to recapture the feeling of those exciting days forty years ago" (p. 1). For a while it seems distantly strange, but the moment he walks out onto what was the taxi strip to photograph his wife it all comes alive; here was the angle at which he'd see things from the nose of his plane, and half a lifetime disappears in seconds.

If these scenes seem familiar, it is because they replicate the opening shots of *Twelve O'Clock High*, the 1949 Twentieth Century-

Fox movie in which Dean Jagger, playing Army Air Force Maj. Harvey Stovall, walks the crumbling, weed-covered runway of what years before had been his heavy bombardment base. Just as in Fred Koger's prologue a certain perspective makes memory shift, and there again are the flights of Flying Fortresses roaring off to bomb Germany in a tragic war of unacceptable attrition. This film, along with *Command Decision* (Metro-Goldwyn-Mayer, 1948), was part of the wave of postwar films that not only questioned the ethics of military command but dramatized the hardship and suffering—not just of crews, but of the leaders. Set in the early days of America's strategic bombing campaign, it not only chose the terms of critical debate but determined images in which the whole matter would be visualized. What for Comer and Koger might be simple nostalgia thus becomes an iconographic portrayal of how the bomber war is remembered by its veterans and represented for later generations.

In Col. Beirne Lay's script, the misfortunes of this bomber war rest most heavily on the group's commander, Gen. Frank Savage, as played by Gregory Peck. Here begins the narrative tradition of witnessing such suffering. Instead of portraying one's self as the victim, memoirists prefer to describe the suffering as others endure it. The perspective begins, of course, with the fighter pilot's view of a bomber going down, but extends through one crew member telling of another's death or wounding or of another crew's loss. Ultimately the witness's tale will focus on the commander, for here lies the final responsibility for sending crews out into a battle where the odds are inescapably against them.

Hollywood's Gen. Frank Savage is no fiction. In book after book commanders emerge as suffering the losses of their men. In editor Ian W. Hawkins's *B-17s Over Berlin* (1990) Capt. John Miller, returning from the disastrous Kiel raid that took the lives of 102 crewmembers from the recently arrived Ninety-fifth Bombardment Group, describes the impact on Col. A.A. Kessler, an old West Pointer not yet fully immersed in the realities of this war's bomber offensive. At the mission's debriefing the colonel listens in stunned silence, "his eyes brimming with tears and very obviously extremely distressed"; all that's heard from their commander is the murmur, to no one in particular, "What's happened to my boys? What's happened to my boys?" (p. 23). In Harry H. Crosby's *A Wing and a Prayer* (1993), Col. Neil Harding fares even worse. As commander of the "Bloody 100th," he absorbs the war's worst losses, his group made special targets by the Luftwaffe after one of its planes, gear down and being escorted to a disabled landing in Germany, opened up on the nearby Messerschmitts and scored several improper kills. On a hard mission to Bremen he flies as command pilot even when far too sick. "I am shocked at how bad he looks" (p. 153), Crosby reports, and later chronicles his hospitalization and relief from command, all due to stress from his group's horrendous losses. A close-up account of such suffering's impact is reported by Jeffrey L. Ethell and Alfred Price in their reconstruction of one day's major operation, *Target Berlin / Mission 250: 6 March 1944* (1989):

> For one crew, bringing back an almost undamaged aircraft, the most heartrending time came after they were safely down. Lieutenant Bob Shoens landed a B-17 "Our Gal Sal" of the 100th Bomb Group at Thorpe Abbotts, one of the few surviving bombers of the ill-fated Low Box of the 13th Wing B formation. Of the twenty B-17s which had taken off, five had broken off the mission early; and 10 out of the remaining 15 had been shot down. Shoens had returned with another box formation. "As we circled the airfield alone we could see a lot of empty spaces. We landed and when we taxied to our space we found our squadron commander waiting for us. He was crying. We were stunned to learn that we were the only aircraft of the squadron to return to the field and only one of four to make it back to England. What do you say, what do you do when your squadron commander is crying and wants to know what has happened? You do the same" (p. 130).

Although fighter squadrons suffered losses too, here is a scene that does not exist in the imagery of fighter jocks and hotshot, competitive commanders. Numbers have something to do with it: when a P-51 goes down, one man at the most dies; a flaming B-17 can take ten crewmen with it. But with the numbers comes responsibility as well. Whereas the fighter pilot might fancy himself as anything from an Arthurian knight (if he's an Anglophile) to a gunslinger from America's Wild West, bomber forces feel differently, especially those in command. There is no Don Blakeslee among them to boast about air combat being the most exciting sporting event of all. Instead, leaders think of themselves more as corporate presidents. This is the comparison that occurs to Col. Beirne Lay near the start of his *I've Had It: The Survival of a Bomb Group Commander* (1945)—not only that his group of seventy-two heavy bombers cost $34 million, but that lives and not just dollars are at stake (p. 2).

A Mustang cost $50,000; a B-17 ten times that, and with ten times the crew on board. No wonder commanding officers cracked under the pressure. And no wonder that everyone, from escorting fighter pilots to crew members at their stations in other ships, paused when a bomber went down. Even the homecoming figured differently. In the melee of dogfighting, P-47s and 51s could be scattered hundreds of miles apart; they often returned singly or in improvised pairs, and although their ground crews waited faithfully for them there was in each case just a single number counted to be assured of safety and success. Far different was the ordeal suffered back at base when the scheduled time for returning B-17s came, for with the sound of the first engines came the start of a hopeful but often desperate counting from one-two-three to thirty-four, thirty-five, thirty-six; and toward the end of the war the numbers swelled to as high as seventy-two. Not that thirty-six or seventy-two was often reached by the pensive control staff and ground crews. Even apart from counts the images can be heartrending, from visibly ragged planes with engines out and features shot away to the disappointment of seeing an otherwise intact B-17 or B-24 firing off a flare to indicate wounded on board.

On his first mission Bert Stiles hears another pilot radio that his navigator has been gravely wounded. There is terror in the man's voice, but Stiles is still bothered by the seeming abstraction of it all, five miles high in his own world: "Up there somewhere in that soft blue sky a navigator was dying. It was pretty hard to believe" (1947, p. 20). Yet all too soon Stiles and others will see death first hand, something the fighter pilots rarely encounter in anything other than technical terms. "Psychologically I saw only the machine," P-51 pilot Leonard Carson writes in *Pursue and Destroy* (1978). "In my mind's eye I never saw the man, only a mechanical entity without a man. The essence of life was not there." When measure is made, it is of a Messerschmitt's or Focke-Wulf's speed and rate of climb, never "the pilot's size or strength . . . how he stood his ground" (p. 87). Indeed, to do so would seem eminently silly. But when in a bomber one of one's own crew is killed or wounded, the human dimension is experienced firsthand.

Wartime publicity efforts skimmed sentimentally over such losses. In *Air Gunner* (1944), Sgt. Bud Hutton and Sgt. Andy Rooney do much like the authors of *Skyways to Berlin*, albeit with a gum-chewing outspokenness that supposedly represents the non-com's point of view. To a man their gunners are self-sacrificing, not just the familiar top-turret man who goes down firing with his ditched ship but a tail gunner who keeps shooting while he bleeds to death rather than calling for help or attending to his wound. No story can exist without suffering or loss; when two gunners on holiday are hosted by some Scots and promise to keep in touch, the episode can't end with happiness—instead, the strange address is found by gunners going through their lost friends' effects, who "figured it probably was some broad" and throw it away (p. 127). A folksy chapter on "the average gunner" ends with his loss on a mission to Emden, which itself stands as an average event. When telling of another gunner's heroic exploits, ones that wound him grievously, the authors even couch news of his reward in terms of suffering and loss: "The doctors think that Forrest Vosler may be able to see enough out of one eye, the right eye, to distinguish the Congressional Medal of Honor they've recommended should be his for the day's work in *Jersey Bounce*" (p. 228). Hutton and Rooney's method throughout has been to make a quick cut from happiness or glory (or even from the routine of average experience) to such matters of impact on the reader. No one can finish *Air Gunner* without feeling that the bomber offensive is less about Germany being torn up than it is about the terrible beating American crews take in the process. Their volume ends with the most touching effect of all, a letter from an unnamed gunner to his parents to be mailed and read only if he's killed or missing in action; because it is being read now, we know the young man has been lost.

Readers, from their necessary distance, can identify with such casualties; mechanisms of sentimentality and pathos allow the losses to be absorbed in a meaningful way. For those more closely on hand, however, it can be a different matter. Intelligence Officer Joseph Florian contributes his reminiscences to *B-17s Over Berlin*, thoughts that are "primarily the view point of a civilian." He tells of the "harsh realities of the air war" being brought home after the Kiel raid of 13 June 1943. Planning has kept him up the night before, debriefing fills much of day itself, and for three hours more he and others wait for missing crews, crews who never return. "These missing men were close friends with whom we'd trained, swapped jokes, laughed, and traveled." As the group is new to combat and still in its original state, these losses "left a void that was impossible to write or think about." Obviously Captain Florian has no need of affecting the reader with these tragedies, for he has been hit hard himself and therefore exists beyond the words that might explain. "Perhaps it sounds callous," he apologizes, "but from that day on I made a silent resolve never to get to know aircrew members as well again, because the heartaches that accompany the sudden loss of such warm friendships were too great to bear" (1990, p. 29).

It is nearly impossible to exaggerate the omnipresence of bomber losses. P-51 pilot Leonard Carson can be cynically detached about it, remarking on how escort duties relieved him of navigation: "You didn't need a compass, just follow the line of burning aircraft to Berlin" (1978, p. 88). As a B-24 navigator himself, John Matt sees the problem a bit differently, yet with equal effect. He thinks of young crewmen awaking morning after morning and when finding themselves posted heading to the flightline for their mission. "There was no corpse-strewn Antietam for them to pass by on the way to their Liberators," he reflects in *Crewdog* (1992), "just that same old yawning abyss which was always there, wider than before." To characterize just what this abyss is like, he lets readers ponder along with him how the very worst might be experienced, when a group is nearly wiped out:

> What would it have been like, I wondered, if that disaster had been inflicted on our group instead, on our first mission, when in the time it takes for a clock's second hand to tick three times around the dial, to have virtually the entire group obliterated; to have Liberators exploding around you or just coming apart, or taking that long, long fall, wrapped in flames, smashing into the ground. To finally make it back to Tibenham alone and thinking you were the only one left, and when the man in the control tower, confused, asks you, "Where is the Group?" and you reply "I am the Group!" What would it have been like to walk into the half-empty living quarters or clubs or mess halls, everyone stunned and quiet, sitting around feeling lucky and guilty and threatened, contemplating your friends' immediate, short past and possibly short future? (p. 121).

One response to the abyss is that of comic fatalism. Early on in *Combat Crew* John Comer learns from a veteran why new crews have only single uniforms: "At the 381st they don't issue any replacement clothes. If you tear your pants, or ruin a blouse, you sweat it out until a gunner your size doesn't make it back" (1988, p. 18). Two months later Comer falls off his bicycle and needs a refit; sure enough, a size thirty-eight gunner fails to return and the author gets new clothes, pausing to express hope that "the unfortunate man got out of the ship in time" (p. 123). Harry Crosby, who after the war became an English professor and in the 1960s would teach Joseph Heller's novel of Air Force absurdities, *Catch-22*, meets an officer straight from Heller's imagination, a man called "Major Minor" (1993, p. 81). Comer himself devises sickly comic routines for whenever new officers arrive at the mess. "Immediately we launched into a morbid discussion of combat raids in drastic detail,

explosions, aircraft fires, dead crewmen, amputations, planes falling in spins out of control," he gleefully reports, making it a point
to act as if these rookies aren't listening. "When the conversation
was particularly gory, there was no sound of knife or fork from the
next table. I noted with satisfaction when we left that the newly arrived officers were no longer hungry" (1988, p. 194). Crosby's
canvas is much broader, allowing him the justifiable claim that "On
August 12, 1943, I made a decision which—I can say without fear of
being contradicted—changed the world" (1993, p. 78). The occasion
is an obscured target, with Crosby's role as lead navigator to choose
a substitute, a so-called target of opportunity. His E6B computer
makes a scientifically logical decision, but it is one the culturally
minded flyer has to reject. "Bonn, Germany," he notes, "a university
town, one of the prettiest places in Germany" (p. 85), which he remembers at once as where Beethoven went to school. "We can't
bomb Bonn," Crosby announces, and explains why. He twirls his
computer again, comes up with a railroad yard in the Ruhr, and directs the pilot there. "A few years later, when our defeated foe
needed a city for its capital, the only large city not leveled by Allied
bombs was Bonn. For whatever reason, we stopped having free-
choice targets of opportunity, and Bonn, though it was nicked a few
times by the British at night, was never bombed by the Americans."
Have Crosby's listening habits altered the course of history? "I can
confidently say that Bonn became the capital of West Germany," he
attests, "because on that night I left the Officers' Club and went to
my barracks and listened to a certain record" (p. 86).

    Yet beyond all tales of suffering and dark comedy are the things
that hold a bomber force together: the immensity of their formations, the attachment to their own planes, and the solidarity of crew
membership itself. The first truly exciting moment in John Comer's
Combat Crew is during the second morning at Bovington, the replacement depot where fresh arrivals from the United States are
sorted out for various stations across eastern England. Here Comer
and his friends are awakened by the roar of many engines. "In a
matter of minutes the barracks were empty," as the young men
tumble out to see an armada of B-17s assembling for a mission.
"The Fortresses were passing overhead on their way to strike the
Mad Dictator, and none of us wanted to miss the sight." How im-
pressive is it? "I have had many thrills in my life," Comer allows,
"but I believe that picture-perfect formation of American bombers
heading for a clash with Goering's best was one of the most emo-
tional experiences I have ever had. I wanted to be up there with

them" (1988, pp. 19-20). For Comer, the scene is exciting enough in its generic potential: the bombers represent America itself, not just on their way to Germany but attacking Adolf Hitler himself, with their Luftwaffe nemesis personalized in the name of its flamboyant leader. But this is indeed the classic way in which the air war was conducted. "Battles had not been fought in tidy formations since the Crimean War," Elmer Bendiner observes in *The Fall of Fortresses* (1980), "but we had been taught that strict formation flying was as vital to us as the British square had been to the infantry" (p. 103). And so the makings of that tight bomber stream heading east at dawn is not just a facile image. It is an effective tactic within the larger strategy that will have Goering living to regret his famous statement that "If an enemy bomber ever flies over Germany, you can call me Meier," and that near the war's end will have bomb loads dropped on Hitler's Berchtesgaden itself.

Other images are more personal. When John Matt and his buddies pick up their new B-24 to fly across the Atlantic, they all admire its state-of-the-art gadgetry and freshness. As opposed to the war weary heaps they've trained in, this plane is pristine, with "no scratches in the flight deck paint, the warning decals all unchipped and readable, the windows and plexiglass domes all diamond clear and un-crazed." It doesn't take a second for the author of *Crewdog* to make the natural connection: "it was like sitting in a new car you just had bought" (1992, p. 92). Collecting his own new B-17 in Oklahoma, Elmer Bendiner takes more time to savor the details, starting with his nickname lettered on the outside of the navigator's station "as it might be on an office door" and continuing with a mix of images telling what proprietorship of this new airplane is like:

> *Tondelayo* had the smell of a new machine. I tried out my desk— a shelf that ran below the gun. I put my head into the astrodome. I peered at the cross hairs of my drift meter. I sat and stood and walked about the nose like a boy given a room to himself. So did we all. This was ours. It was a home of our own, a car of our own, a ship of our own. Her engines quickly took on a special sound unlike all other engines. We stood back and looked at her as horsemen look at the lines of a thoroughbred. We liked the way she lifted her tail. We admired her gleaming flanks. We watched her from the ground on her test flights. We followed her as she took off, climbed and wheeled, flinging back the sun. One B-17 is not like another. Each has its crochets and graces. Once it has absorbed its share of lives and deaths it can live, be loved and die (1980, p. 58).

In less than one paragraph Bendiner takes both his men and their fresh new plane through an entire cycle. It's like getting a new car, but more than that: from ship and horse to room and home the range covers a broad expanse of a person's life, just as the imprint of those lives makes the plane an almost living thing. Living, and eventually dying—all in a cycle that draws its merit from the natural order of existence. In Bendiner's first sentence the aircraft is born as a piece of machinery; in his last it dies a fitting death. No wonder few crewmen can look without emotion at those pictures from 1946 and 1947 of hundreds of B-17s lined up in the Arizona desert, waiting for dismantling and the smelter. A part of them dies with each plane as well.

Like the aircraft they fly, crews have their own identity: not just a corporate mass, but a mathematical factor in which the total is quite literally more than the sum of its parts. That each entity is a full, living human being makes this inevitable. There is an infinity of possible associations based on each man's personality and background. The key to success is finding ten such men who will work well together.

In RAF Bomber Command crewing up was left to the crew members themselves. After finishing their individual courses and just before being posted to an operational training unit, pilots, navigators, bomb-aimers, radio operators, and gunners were expected to form their own seven-man units (for such comprised the full crew of a Lancaster bomber). Sometimes this would happen under direct orders in a large hall or hangar, individuals moving about and eyeing each other like potential partners at a dance. In Don Charlwood's *Journeys into Night* (1991) the author and his batch of trainees anticipate the move and begin forming up on their own. In doing so they follow implicitly the practice the RAF is counting on: that by subtle nuances of psychology and intuition those who can work well together will be mutually attracted. This is just what happens to Charlwood. He's a bit nervous about the process, fearful that "trying to judge who would prove a 'good' pilot was beyond rational judgment" (p. 75). These fears are shared with a pilot who turns out to feel the same way, and the first match is made. From this pilot-navigator keystone the remaining relationships are formed, based on more logical criteria (an all-non-commissioned officer [NCO] crew, for example, so that they would live and mess together; gunnery scores; and so forth). Charlwood's story and the memoirs of others in Bomber Command indicate that on the whole this was a good practice. After all, the crews would be isolated together as in no other branch of the service—not just in their bombers but alone in the night, where formation flying was impossible. Such crews "were entering the most interdependent relationship of their lives, brief though it usually turned out to be," the author notes. "Even if they survived, they would be disbanded in their moment of triumph, probably never again to fly together, some never again to see each other. But these things were not yet known to us. What we *did* know was that each crew was an independent entity, which would find its own way to the target" (p. 76). In *Pathfinders* (1946), Wing Commander William Anderson describes the magic of this meld. "Seven men, very much alone together in the night, meanness, greed, and jealousy swept away by the keen air of danger, are welded by fire into one." By functioning as a unit in such circumstances "Each loses himself in the crew and so finds himself, curiously secure in spite of danger, comforted in spite of difficulties, somehow safe and at peace in the middle of death and destruction" (p. 18).

With its shoals of staff psychologists and vast numbers of trainees, the USAAF relied on a more scientific method of crew selection, although with the same results in mind. Just as the Eagle squadron pilots revised RAF styles of fighter-pilot heroism earlier in the war, so crewing took on a new dimension. At the end of "Mister," the first half of Eugene Fletcher's *The Lucky Bastard Club* (1993) which is devoted to the author's training as a pilot, the formation of crews is described. Here in the modern world of American efficiency, where everything is new and improved by the wonders of technology and science, crews are formed on the basis of psychological tests and sociological indices. "People were assigned in a manner designed to avoid personality clashes," Fletcher writes. "One member of the crew must have Type O blood, a universal donor, and no more than two people from the same state could be on one crew" (pp. 218-19). Working for the War Department and the Army Air Force itself, novelist John Steinbeck used his own skills as an artificer of plot and character to convince potential recruits just how well their crew would work together. "This is the kind of organization that Americans above all others are best capable of maintaining," he argues in *Bombs Away: The Story of a Bomber Team* (1942), because "here is no commander with subordinates, but a group of responsible individuals functioning as a unit while each member exercises individual judgment and foresight and care" (p. 23). In supporting this argument, Steinbeck draws on everything from science to mythology. He moves from the psychologist's clinic to movie-house images of popular culture, on the one hand assuring prospective crew members that they've been screened for their tasks by the most sophisticated and foolproof test-

ing ever devised, while on the other justifying a flight engineer's apti-
tude based on his reputation as the neighborhood Mr. Fix-It and a
pilot's qualification on his teen-aged expertise with hot cars. Sports
metaphors abound: not everyone on a football team insists on being
the quarterback, team players must have initiative combined with
group spirit, and so forth.

Beyond the patriotism and propaganda, Steinbeck does explain
the interactive nature of a bomber crew. It is not all the pilot's show,
he emphasizes convincingly. "Just as the ship is a highly complicated unit, so the air crew is considered as a unit, each member of
which is equally important" (p. 114). Modern times make this even
more so, as "the Air Force is an association of experts and each
must place a dependence on the other" (p. 152). To prove his point
the novelist takes his sample crew, each member of which has had
his own introductory chapter, and sends them on a training mission
where by dint of everyone's unique expertise a German submarine is
tracked, sighted, and sunk, resulting in a single action that "welds"
them together (p. 163). The result is the same fusion remarked by
RAF authors Don Charlwood and William Anderson and countless
other memoirists of Bomber Command. But the process of achieving
it has been much different, trusting not to the impromptu affinities
of strangers in a huge hall but to a combination of testing and popular stereotyping. The latter two work hand in hand, as test scores
satisfy the clipboard specialists while general readers find themselves feeling as comfortable as viewing an Andy Hardy movie or
thinking about the kid next door.

So much importance is attached to crew spirit that when it is
missing a gloominess takes over. There is little happiness in the first
half of Bert Stiles's *Serenade to the Big Bird* because the author's
crew is not jelling. His appraisal is as acute as John Steinbeck's, yet
more telling because it's made without a push for good morale behind
it, rather with an admission of how morale can fail:

> From the time you're a little kid, you dream about being with a
> bunch of guys, who by working together, and just being together,
> give each other something that makes them more than just a
> bunch of guys.
>   It makes them a team.
>   And somehow we didn't have it.
>   A great crew is just about as rare a thing as a great ball team.
> They just come along once in a while. There isn't much you can
> do about it, if you're not, I guess. It's a spontaneous thing.
>   We were average, better than some, lazier than most (1947,
> p. 86).

In this real world beyond the bell curve of optimum testing and well past the stuff of happy-ending movies Bert Stiles's crew plods on, not even sure that they're making the best of it. His pilot doesn't care for the responsibility of leading a crew, but Stiles can't lay blame; he's not a very good copilot himself because he'd rather be in Mustangs. Their navigator "didn't give a damn about being a lead navigator," the goal of most achievers. "He just wanted to live, just wanted to get through and go back to running around" (p. 87). The bombardier lacks confidence. The enlisted men, off at their gunnery stations, are "just there" (p. 88). As a crew, the most that can be said is that they get back every time. But without great heroics or fine bonding. "Our crew didn't really belong in the war," Stiles figures. "We'd never really acclimated. We were just ten guys involved in a war" (p. 90).

Stiles's inversion of Steinbeck's imagery is almost complete. The team spirit Steinbeck has described is that of a winning team, a great team. Stiles's crew mates aren't losers, they finish in the pack, but are far from being champions. As for popular types, they qualify, but from somewhere else in the cast of characters: not the mechanical genius tinkering with jalopies or the wizard ham radio operator down the block, but the young man good with ladies, always messing around to the exclusion of anything else.

Yet there is one factor from *Bombs Away* that Stiles can't invert, and that is the bonding under stress that characterizes any crew coming through true adversity. In *Serenade to the Big Bird* such compelling danger doesn't happen until near the end, when all the elements of a hard air war come together. The target is a distant one, Leipzig. Aerial opposition is extremely heavy, up to 200 German fighters using the new "company front" tactic of massing in lines six abreast and ten deep coming at the bomber formation head on, then circling around to repeat this action half a dozen times more. There's a Mustang escort, but a small one, outnumbered twenty-five to one. A squadron just ahead, manned by some of Stiles's closest friends, is badly mauled, virtually wiped out. The single positive is that Stiles's plane has a new pilot, and so there's none of the uncomfortableness that had dogged the cockpit before. Now they work well together, the pilot able to call for extra power when he needs it, the copilot confident that he can supply it properly. The gunners do their own jobs well. Bombs are placed on target, while good navigation and radio work promise that they'll have a safe return. Clear of flak and fighters and with their bomb load delivered, the crew has done its job and can begin working for itself—as a crew, that is, for it is the melded specialties of each that will bring them back safely. And what a wonderful feeling that is:

> The sky was a soft unbelievable blue. The land was green, never so green.
> When we got away from the Continent we began to come apart. Green took off his mask.
> There weren't any words, but we tried to say them.
> "Jesus, you're here," I said.
> "I'm awfully proud of them," he said quietly.
> Bradley came down out of the turret. His face was nothing but teeth. I mussed up his hair, and he beat on me.
> The interphone was jammed.
> " . . . all I could do was pray . . . and keep praying." McAvoy had to stay in the radio room the whole time, seeing nothing, doing nothing. . . .
> "You can be the chaplain," Mock said. His voice was just the same, only he was laughing a little now (p. 157).

Better crewed and having fought his way through trouble, Bert Stiles can write a scene equal to John Steinbeck's fiction, motivated by the truth that these happenings and the emotions behind them are real.

Performance and not pretested psychology is what makes a crew work well together. In *A Wing and a Prayer* rookie navigator Harry Crosby has some doubts about his pilot, especially after he's had trouble starting the engines for their first mission. But when their assembly slot is taken and the pilot speaks up firmly for their space—and by dint of commanding presence gets it—the author is convinced enough to pen his decision that "I will fly with him anywhere" (1993, p. 48).

Each crew station has its unique dangers. Given the Luftwaffe's success with head-on attacks, pilot and copilot were likely to be the initial targets. Flying tight formation, there would be little room for maneuver, and the encounters themselves, at closing speeds in excess of 500 mph, allowed little time for reaction, especially as the opposing fighters could begin firing with accuracy from as far as 300 yards out. Collisions were a possibility, thanks to misjudgment or a German flyer being hit and killed on his run in. Often an Me-109 or FW-190 would pass inches away, its pilot slumped forward over jammed controls. Intentional rammings were not unheard of, as pilot David Shellhamer reports in Brian D. O'Neill's *Half a Wing, Three Engines, and a Prayer: B-17s Over Germany* (1989). "He was not firing at all when he was well within his own range," Shellhamer says of a Focke-Wulf pilot closing from ahead. The B-17 pilot eases his aircraft down, but so does the German. "It required split-second timing, but my timing was good," the American attests, because at the last minute he pulls the bomber up while the speeding fighter shoots fifty feet beneath. "I will never forget the green scarf that German pilot had around his neck" (p. 102), Shellhamer insists, remembering the type of scene so many pilots witnessed during these company front assaults.

Even closer to the front are navigator and bombardier, especially so in the plexiglass B-17 nose. Here a flak hit could take off the nose entirely, right where assemblers at the Boeing plant had bolted it to the plane's fuselage. The bomber could still fly this way, and noseless Fortresses that limped back to base would be pointed out as objects of wonder. But if navigator and bombardier were at their stations, as inevitable during a bombing run when flak was worst, there was no way either could survive such a hit.

Among enlisted men crew responsibilities involved their own special dangers. The radio man worked out of sight, but without any practical protection, as the aluminum skin of a Fortress or Liberator was as light and thin as possible. Sitting just behind the highly explosive oxygen tanks, he was a bomb waiting to go off. A flight engineer would have his own special risks, as John Comer describes in *Combat Crew*:

> When there was a hung-up bomb or two it was my signal to go into the high-wire bomb-releasing act on the ten-inch catwalk between the radio room and the rear cockpit door. Two vertical supporting beams halfway between the two doors restricted the walk-through space so severely that it was almost impossible to get through it wearing a parachute. So I had to work on the narrow walk without a chute; it was like a high-wire performer with no safety net. Oxygen supply was from an unreliable walk-around bottle good for four minutes with no bodily exertion or excitement that could double the need for oxygen. An oxygen failure on that open walk, with nothing below but five miles of air, was something I tried not to think about (1988, p. 72).

On earlier B-17 models—the ones where bombs hung up the most—there was also adversity for the waist gunners, as these planes had no doors to break the subzero wind and chill. True, suits were electrically heated and the gunners wore heavy gloves, but they came off for clearing a jam and sometimes in the frenzy of combat could not be put back on. These waist gunners also faced the worst mortality rates; planners fond of actuarial charts calculated that their average life expectancy was three minutes of firing time—not much, even considering the optimum burst was a couple of seconds or less.

Tail gunners had it bad too. Any fighter approaching from the rear, a favored tactic early in the war, would strive to knock this man out with his initial attack, leaving the bomber undefended for more calculated slaughter. If the interphone were jammed or knocked out, as often happened when a plane took heavy hits, the tail gunner couldn't hear bailout orders; only by wiggling himself around to get an angled view of the wings and rear fuselage might he guess if it were time to abandon ship. Plus he could be isolated in another, even more frightening way. Just as the plexiglass nose of a B-17 could be blown completely off, so was it possible for the entire tail section of this mighty bomber to break free. Here there was a chance of survival, if terrifyingly so. More than one story has been told of a gunner riding his tail section all the way down, thanks to the happenstance of its aerodynamic stability. One version has the brave gunner continuing to fire away at a pursuing Messerschmitt, perhaps not aware that he's the sole quarry; a variation confirms the gunner's blithe ignorance, easily surviving what he assumes to be the softest forced landing ever only to open his door and find absolutely no evidence of the plane.

Most gruesome of all could be the fate suffered by a ball turret gunner. Unless he were exceptionally small, he could not fit into the turret with his parachute; it had to be kept up in the fuselage, retrieved at the moment of need. The turret itself had to be turnable to a special position for entrance and egress; if it jammed, the only way out was to be rescued on the ground, after a landing with just a few inches for clearance. But if a turret were jammed from combat damage, it was more than likely that the plane's undercarriage was useless as well; again, more than one story tells of a gunner resigning himself to a horrible death when his plane has to belly in, himself trapped beneath. Even being shot at his crew station could be nasty for those who had to clean up, explosive shells leaving so little of a body intact that the remains had to be washed away with a high-pressure hose.

No wonder pilot Eugene Fletcher takes his role as leader so seriously. Early in *Fletcher's Gang* (1988) he writes to his wife about how busy he's been during the final stage of training. Fully schooled as individuals, this fresh assemblage of men, in groups of ten each, must learn to function together. From copilot to tail gunner, he finds, "they are concerned only with the worries and responsibilities which affect their own position." Not so for the pilot: "In my case I'm concerned with the worries and have responsibility of all ten positions. I can't quite explain how it works, but the pilot is held responsible for everything that affects his crew" (p. 27). Hence even at this stage, long before the adversities of combat, he must concern himself with strategies to help his crew do their separate jobs better and hence build confidence toward working as a group. These comments are made in April 1944; by November Fletcher's gang has become solidly joined and are referring to themselves as one, testimony that their pilot's methods have worked. "The crew is still one happy family," he writes just before their thirtieth of thirty-five missions, "and now we air our thoughts freely with one another and depend more on one another as time goes by." No small part of this is that "I'm the 'Old Rock' they can cling to to keep their thinking straight while being unnerved by their existence here." Little do his men know that he's as much or more homesick than all of them. "But it's my job, and since my neck depends on their actions they will never know my feelings" (p. 208). Such concerns are referred to frequently, and constitute a structuring rhythm for the book.

Crew identity had time to build. A twenty-five-mission tour could last five to seven months in 1943, given the pounding unescorted bombers took and the need to recover and regroup. When in 1944 long-range escorts and a weaker Luftwaffe made missions somewhat less dangerous, quotas were raised to thirty and then to thirty-five, keeping both time span and survival odds about the same. In telling their stories about these tours, bomber veterans have their own ways of shaping the narrative. For Eugene Fletcher in *Fletcher's Gang*, the organizing principles are simple: the nature of his own responsibility as leader versus the countdown he keeps in his letters home, hoping that his tour will be completed by Christmas—he succeeds at the former, and in being slightly disappointed in the latter gains the final measures of maturity and resolve that help him do his duties to the end. In *Combat Crew* John Comer's structures are more homely and comic, as he makes a practice of lurking outside the closed doors of navigator briefings and measuring distance and difficulty of targets according to how long and loud are the moans. As far as his crew duties are concerned, he rarely lets a mission or a chapter pass without tinkering with some piece of equipment to make it work better; here at last is John Steinbeck's archetypal Mr. Fix-It from *Bombs Away*. Harry Crosby's *A Wing and a Prayer* is shaped somewhat as a coming-of-age novel, his own incompetence at navigation being put to a tempering test that he passes and thus becomes a master. Another typical tale is that of the hard-as-nails, wring-out-the-best-performance leader, best told by Maj. Gen. Dale O. Smith III in *Screaming Eagle*. Asked to take over a hard luck, low-morale outfit, Smith comes in as group commander and instills a discipline previously unheard of in these quarters. Takeoffs are done by strict order of stopwatch and flares; pilots flying in too loose formation are docked credit for the mission; returning bombers must overfly the field in tight order, being graded on their relative proficiency; lead ships piloted by commanders have the bumped pilot stationed in the tail, reporting from the gunner's position on how tight the bomber stream is boxed. On the plus side, flying and ground messes are integrated, better cooking is encouraged, and ice-cream making facilities are acquired. By steps such as these is Smith's story organized, with spectacular bombing achieved almost as a matter of course.

The importance of crew identity for all these narratives is confirmed in Keith Schuyler's *Elusive Horizons* (1969). For several reasons he and his mates feel excluded. First of all, they fly a B-24 Liberator, a plane they love and respect but which has been given worse than second billing by Air Force publicists and war correspondents conditioned to see the bomber war as fought from B-17s. Second, Schuyler's is a replacement crew, something he describes as "a lonely entity." The reasons why are human and understandable. "It was accepted to take over a spot which might have belonged to one of the old gang who had earned a certain affection and respect." The former crew may have at best gone home, might be confined to a POW camp, or at worst been killed in action. "In any event, it had left a void that no replacement crew could possibly deserve [to fill] until it earned it" (p. 13).

Alienation sets the tone. Given a new B-24 right off the assembly line, Schuyler's crew proudly takes it across the Atlantic as their first act of real business. None of them will ever forget the plane, least of all Schuyler, who has named it "Sweet Eloise," after his wife, paying a GI artist seven dollars in Marrakesh for the inscription. But "the moment we set foot on the ground again, they took her from us. We were just a replacement crew" (p. 8). Hence when after many missions in borrowed planes and as fill-in for others these flyers finally receive their own aircraft and are dispatched as a regular part of the raid, their captain gets "a good feeling inside," as though for the first time he and his men are "a part of the 44th; and more importantly, that someone cared" (p. 106). It is only in this framework, of having a recognizable part in the war, that the crew's work seems meaningful, a feeling that rebounds among the crew itself as team loyalty—to the extent that when Schuyler recommends his copilot for a plane of his own, the man declines, wishing to say with his cohort.

Such affinity is common. When at the end of *Combat Crew* John Comer finished up ahead of his crew mates, he sees them off on a mission with the feeling that he "almost wished I was going with them" (1988, p. 281). In some cases, tour-expired crew members actually did. When Comer ships home, he's overtaken by a vision of his buddies, a vision that he can only reconcile by religious faith:

> More than anything, I saw Jim and George, I could almost hear their voices, those comically contrasting accents of the Bronx and Mississippi. We had shared a unique and special brotherhood, forged by circumstances and tested by adversity. It was a gift of friendship beyond anything I had experienced before. And I knew it could not be replaced.
>
> As I remembered them, I felt an overwhelming sadness, and turned away from the others nearby to hide the tears that I could not blink away. At that moment I experienced an intuition of startling clarity. Suddenly I realized that we would meet again. I did not know how or when, but I knew! "Death is not the end, but only the beginning of a new dimension." How many times had I heard that Christian refrain? But I suppose that I had never fully accepted its meaning until that moment. There was no longer any doubt. I felt a certainty and a peace. The sense of gloom lifted and I was a different person (p. 285).

The remarkable truth is that such meetings do happen—not yet verifiably in the afterlife, but in the practical equivalent of crew reunions in the radically different dimension of postwar, late middle-aged existence. Who cannot be fascinated by the striking juxtaposition of photographs: two ranks of smartly uniformed or flight-jacketed young men positioned in front of their B-17 or B-24, then a group of seventy-year-olds in sports shirts and golf pants gathered around a sofa, every neighborhood's old guy out there with his rake or watering the shrubs, except that these old guys flew thirty missions over Hitler's Europe and came back. How wonderful when there are still ten of them to gather today.

This is how *Fletcher's Gang* concludes. In January 1945 the author is surprised at how hard parting is. "Sure hated to see them go, in a way," writes this man who has been counting down the days left before he can ship home to his wife and newborn child. "We had been through a lot together. I bid them good-bye in London, a rather touching ordeal. After all we'd done it seemed kind of odd to see them with tears in their eyes—and in mine too." His contemporaneous assessment is a telling one: "A finer bunch of fellows will never be found again on one crew. I sure enjoyed having them with me. But every pilot thinks he has the best crew there is" (1988, p. 246), which is just the strategy intended from John Steinbeck's *Bombs Away* and all of the Air Force planning for crews. Thus when at the end of Eugene Fletcher's book his crew has its first reunion in forty-one years, the author enjoys taking responsibility for giving the customary update of what each fellow has done in the afterlife that followed the war. "All members present or accounted for, Sir," the old B-17 pilot proudly reports. "Crew dismissed!"

The religious dimension of the bomber crew experience has an epistemological counterpart in the way these flyers learned about their war. No one person, whether in a Mustang or a Flying Fortress, could have an overall picture of what was happening as it transpired. Missions were flown to individual targets; other bomb groups would be hitting elsewhere, so the only way to get an overall picture was to compare notes—a slow, laborious, and jigsaw-puzzle-like endeavor that did not always yield accurate results. Neither could a solitary crew member be aware of everything that happened on his aircraft. With their various concerns, pilots in the cockpit fought a different war than bombardiers and navigators up in the nose, where calculating drift and steadying up for the Initial Point of a bombing run took precedence over matters of trim and power. Gunners had a radically different perspective: physically from their positions above, below, behind, and at the sides of the plane, and mentally because theirs was the role of defending it all from fighter assault. Information could be exchanged by interphone, and afterwards their experiences could be compared. Little by little a fuller picture took form. It might not be complete, but when assembled it offered a more comprehensive view than available to the fighter jock doing his own thing among a squadron of colleagues doing pretty much the same, the only variations being between flying lead or wing.

Hence descriptions of the bombers' war are shaped with group experience in mind. Where fighter pilots see incisive action, bomber crew members illustrate with deeper range, forever questing for the big picture that the conditions of their storytelling make hypothetically possible. A Thunderbolt ace such as Robert S. Johnson looks at bombers and sees individual planes being shot down. As one who flies in B-17s himself, navigator Elmer Bendiner views things differently. Even when his *Fall of Fortresses* approaches its conclusion as his combat tour nears completion, he still has to pause in wonderment as hundreds of bombers gather in formations before heading toward Germany. "I caught my breath when from our position in the high squadron I saw again the great spectacle of a mighty fleet of Fortresses making white tracks in the blue sky," he writes, "their shadows dancing over mountains of cloud below" (1980, p. 219).

Given that it is the great mass of a bombing force that makes for its effectiveness, memoirists take special note when a plane distinguishes itself—not one of a string of incidents being observed by a fighter pilot well above the stream, but a suddenly personal incident happening to someone squarely in it. During one of his own assembly descriptions Harry Crosby complains of zero visibility; there will be no grand accounts such as Bendiner's here. Then he's startled by the choppiness their plane encounters, propwash indicating that another craft is near. "Suddenly, from the front and starboard, a squadron of Liberators flew right through our formation," the surprised observer reports. "I saw B-24 navigators and bombardiers, their mouths open—they must have been yelling—and their arms up and around their heads, instinctively trying for protection" (1993, p. 157).

Crosby is lucky: midair collisions did happen, an average of one a day during the heavy mission crushes of 1944, and in *Elusive Horizons* Keith Schuyler reserves his most vivid writing for just such an occasion. As with Crosby's account, the weather is far from ideal, this time with a front moving in and only a few clear spaces left in which planes can maneuver with clear visibility, albeit in light that is rapidly fading as huge cloud banks build up on either side. "All at once," Schuyler sees with alarm, "the dim sky split apart in the monumental crash of a giant fireball." In the gathering darkness the effect is hellish, as "this sudden sun of red-black flame splashed its hue against every airplane and the walls of mist for miles around." Then the spectacle recedes, fireball into flames, flames into smoke, a "sphere that hovered in place, a dirty, dark monument to twenty men and two great bombers now shredded to bits." Those bits themselves are worthy of special description:

> Below the ball, some of the bits dropped swiftly as tiny blobs of debris. A few larger ones, still flaming, undulated downward, their descent marked by a twisting spiral of thin black smoke. Somehow, unbelievably, out of the debris blossomed five parachutes. We could only morbidly surmise what the harnesses below the white umbrellas now held. Over 5,000 gallons of high test gasoline and 10,400 pounds of incendiary bombs had been in those two airplanes.

Within seconds, flame from the ground indicated that not all the incendiaries had exploded aloft. The collision had occurred over an air base. One end of a hangar was burning fiercely. There were other fires, too (1992, p. 33).

Keith Schuyler's story is shaped as only a bomber veteran's can be. To him, there is nothing anonymous about a formation or its assembly; each, like a crew itself and the large, complex aircraft it flies, is put together with forethought and care. And even though all will contend as large forces, components can still act with the subtlest of nuances, be they the airplanes in flight or the weather itself. Even an element of fire has its own life, coloring aircraft and atmosphere alike. It is when things malfunction and consequently burst apart that a writer such as Schuyler can see how this act unveils the larger picture: of two planes that even in their mass destruction can be seen to have carried ten men each plus specific loads of fuel and ordnance. And not just from anywhere, but from an airbase such as the whole grand enterprise has been confounded to partially destroy. The narrative expands, contracts, particularizes itself, and then circles back just like the faulty formation, its very assembly undoing itself—deconstructing itself—before the reader's eyes.

When bombers fall, writers from other crews particularize. In *B-17s Over Berlin* navigator James F. Goff tells how Fortresses took off at strict thirty-second intervals. Next in line, he watches from his plane's plexiglass nose as the B-17 ahead gets only halfway down the runway before banking to the left, falling, and exploding in the same ball of fire and black smoke that characterized Keith Schuyler's report. But the controller's stopwatch counts on, and in half a minute Goff finds himself passing "directly over the crashed bomber at 100-foot altitude." Looking down, "I could see the entire Fortress engulfed in flames. There couldn't possibly be any survivors from that fiery hell" (1990, p. 121). Anonymous as the massive bomber war might be, there are always particularizing incidents such as these to remind the crew member just how vulnerable he is. The planes Schuyler sees collide are forming up according to the same type of plan he himself is following, over the same buncher beacon whose radio signal helps them measure their distance apart; Goff's B-17 is carrying the same overload of fuel and bombs that tips its immediate predecessor out of control. Just getting up and down can be dicey. Contrasting notes of tension and ease distinguish Fred Koger's story of taking off one day in *Countdown!*: "I tried to recall what the weather officer had said about base conditions for our return, but couldn't remember." That's a matter for concern, for he's just observed that takeoffs and landings are his two chief worries. "Oh well, I thought, they sure as hell wouldn't have sent us out if there was no place to land when we got back," a little mantra meant to make himself relax. "But that's *exactly* what they did," he reveals in a one sentence paragraph that stands threateningly by itself. Roaring on through the fog and darkness, there's no visibility for the longest time, even as he peers through his bombardier's plexiglass to watch for other planes, "though I knew that if I saw one it would probably be just before we collided." Finally, after all this push and pull of contrary emotions, "we broke through into the bright blue morning sky and the tenseness went out of my body in a sudden surge" (1990, p. 161). The most frightening accidents, it seems, are the one's that don't happen, but that easily could.

Then there are the actual losses. Fighter attacks happen so suddenly that they are hard to believe; human comprehension cannot absorb their reality except in terms borrowed from other aspects of life. "Those unreal fighters, beautiful as swift arrows, came at us again in twos and threes," Elmer Bendiner observes. Gunners call out the tracks, but from his navigator's position in the nose the author can see them "only when they came head on, flashing, turning and exiting in marvelous choreography. The impersonal quality of the menace was eerie. It was as if I were in battle with beautiful birds of prey" (1980, p. 100). From far away bombers that are lost do seem anonymous, especially when taken out by flak. In *Fletcher's Gang* a B-17 up ahead suffers a direct hit and "disappeared into thin air. All that remained was a larger smoke cloud and a few burning streamers floated earthward" (1988, p. 68). But when Fred Koger sees a flak burst catch a plane in close formation, matters are starkly real, if hardly more believable. "I heard a 'pop' that sounded like a faraway pistol shot and felt a sudden warmth on my face," he notices just as he adjusts his sight for the bomb run. "What the hell was going on? My eyes snapped to the right, and there was Crosby's B-17 . . . upside down!" His bombardier's concentration broken, Koger cannot help his fascination with the challenging picture just yards away. "Jesus," he exclaims, "the right wing was *gone*! Completely gone! I continued to stare, and couldn't believe what I was seeing. A B-17 upside down! Then I saw the harsh red flames streaking back from where the wing used to be, blurring the shape of the fuselage." No longer functioning as a bomber and hardly an airplane at all, nevertheless "for an eternity the doomed B-17 seemed to hang there as if it wanted to stay with the formation. Then it started to slide away, and in an instant it was gone" (1990, p. 12).

In close-at-hand experiences such as this, odd things happen to normal dimensions of existence. Space collapses; time stands still; motion suspends itself as if hanging there for the observer to assimilate, then at the moment of recognition shoots off into another realm, that of time past and death. Again, the witness strives to personalize. For Bert Stiles, the image of a Fortress being hit is that of "a great wound" having "opened up" (1947, p. 66). In *Bomber Pilot* (1978) Philip Ardery has a stricken B-24 pull up right in front of him, its fuselage swept with flames. "As we went by and under it," he describes, "we could see it glowing like the inside of a furnace" (p. 126). When another B-24 bursts into fire in the same box formation as Keith Schuyler, he's drawn to help the dying men, helpless as he is to do so. Transfixed, he can't take his eyes from it. Finally, "at the top of the wingover, the doomed B-24 gave up. It didn't blow; it just melted apart. Like a bird caught by a blast of shot, the heavy parts fell first, and feathers of debris followed in a long string of smoking wreckage." And after that: nothing at all, just a return to blue sky. "An empty, beautiful blue. Empty of a great bomber and ten men" (1992, p. 45), just as if they'd never been there at all.

From close up or far away, however, the spectacle can be too much to handle. These are very young men, after all, the officers perhaps twenty-one to twenty-three years old, the non-coms nineteen or twenty—any twenty-six-year-old on a crew earns the inevitable nickname of "Pops." Nor have these members of a bomber crew had tough or violent lives; training and background, and often times historical fact, make them more like a university's sophomore and junior classes than a gang of street fighters from the school of hard knocks. What heavy action they've seen has been in the movies, and therefore it's from the cinema that they draw images to explain their experience—not just pictures from the screen, but the entire situation of watching such action with a box of popcorn on one's lap and a girlfriend cuddling beside.

"I wonder if there has ever been a sight—show or drama—as thrilling as watching a series of dog fights between good pilots, with all of them aware that death awaited the losers," John Comer speculates from his top-turret position in *Combat Crew*. "It was such a fascinating sight I sometimes forgot briefly that I was part of the drama. At times I almost felt like it was a highly realistic war movie in which I was a bit player" (1988, p. 74). When not a lead navigator and thus assigned to full-time watch from the nose gun position, Harry Crosby can't even imagine himself as a supporting character in the film. "I don't feel real," he complains. "This is a movie, not me.

I am watching. It is not happening to me" (1993, p. 42). But it surely is, and soon enough action develops that has both authors painting vivid word pictures in attempts to capture the scene. Yet even here the reminder is of unfolding narrative, and if there's any doubt about it, all they need do is look down from their returning bombers to see this action's denouement lying there before them like pages dropped from the script. "All across Germany, Holland, and Belgium," Elmer Bendiner writes, "the terrible landscape of burning planes unrolled beneath us. It seemed that we were littering Europe with our dead. We endured this awesome spectacle while we suffered a desperate chill." The stage is indeed littered like the final scene of *Hamlet*, and Bendiner for one can feel as in character as the most convincing Shakespearean actor, even though he's had no direct part in the killing, just guiding a bomb load to an unseen target and firing tracerless ammunition at fighters flashing past so quickly as to seem unreal. "The cartridge casings were filling our nose compartment up to our ankles," he notes, adding that there's no doubt whatsoever about himself being here. "My flak vest grew heavier as we proceeded until it seemed that I could survive everything but that weight or armor and the cold that twisted my guts" (1980, p. 174).

What was the sense of achievement a bomber crew might feel? Certainly it was different from that of the fighter pilot, whose successes let him fancy himself a fighter jock and act that way even when away from flying. The RAF, its bombing offensive having geared up well before the Americans', offers some clues, such as a British gunnery officer on temporary assignment to a B-24 unit who flies with Philip Ardery in *Bomber Pilot*. "I don't know how others feel about this bloody business," he confides. "But when I see the bomb doors open and I hear the bombardier call 'bombs away' over the intercom, I get a thrill that's almost sexual in its intensity" (1978, p. 85). The flight lieutenant's instincts are correct, above all in artistic effect; novelist John Steinbeck titled his introductory volume *Bombs Away* precisely for the climactic excitement of this phrase. Eugene Fletcher agrees, and in *Fletcher's Gang* characterizes it as "that spine-chilling rumble caused by the open bomb-bay doors" that can be heard even "above the engines' thunder" (1988, p. 85). "Somehow, after you've dropped your bombs," believes Keith Schuyler, "you get the feeling that everything is all right" (1992, p. 136). Perhaps the truest but also most self-indicting judgment comes from gunner Ben Smith, Jr., who in *Chick's Crew* (1978) sees his plane's load of incendiaries dropped into the "hell's cauldron" of a blazing refinery. "Suddenly as I gazed out on this," he reflects, "a feeling of exaltation swept over me. It was magnificent. I had the sudden revelation: This would not be happening if men didn't love it" (p. 99).

At the very least, such doings put the little, normal things of life into better perspective. "The next morning it was great to awake at a reasonable hour and look forward to a day of unruffled simplicity," John Comer suggests in *Combat Crew*. "The morning after a rough raid I always felt in tune with the universe. I had once again thumbed my nose at the odds and was still there." Even menial tasks now seem wonderful, and Comer the eternal tinkerer looks forward to losing himself in the "small, everyday tasks" such as polishing shoes and repairing equipment, all of which are now contemplated with pleasure. "When one lives on the brink of extinction," he reasons, "his outlook on life undergoes a change, for he realizes that life is a fragile and precious gift. I had a full day at my disposal and I intended to enjoy every moment of it" (1988, pp. 109-10).

There are moments on operations when during quiet intervals mundane things become wonderful. Breaking through a towering overcast into sudden sunlight, with silvery B-17s popping up all around—many memoirists have noted this feature which transforms the labor of a zero-visibility assembly into a moment of grand pleasure. Taking off in clear skies but before dawn, as often happens, yields another delight: seeing how different a sunrise looks when observed from high aloft. Even tight formation flying offers the experience of seeing planes on either side bob gently up and down, a reminder that these mighty craft are indeed air*ships*.

It's always a happy time when a mission's escort shows up; once those escorts are Mustangs, with range all the way to Berlin, the feeling is joyful indeed. One such moment is described by John Matt in *Crewdog* on returning from the marshaling yards at Hamm, a heavily defended target that becomes doubly hard when the formation leader demands a second bomb run. Afterwards, German fighters gather at the rally point to attack the regathering formations, but by the time Holland is reached this opposition has fallen away. When the first Mustangs from their escort home show up, the day's work seems safely in the bag, and from his navigator's position in the nose Matt pauses to enjoy the sight.

The fighters "patrolled above us in lazy, sweeping arcs," he observes. "Our relative motions gave them a grace and apparent speed which was as unreal as it was beautiful." This sense of quiet beauty is shared, for in his earphones Matt hears someone in the formation

call out, "Hey, little friend, how about a slow roll?" Surely an innocent request, and a nearby Mustang pilot, doubtless as happy as the
bomber crew, is pleased to comply. But note with the author what
happens, just when everything seems to be going so well:

> One of the fighters above us suddenly swept up into a beautiful,
> precise roll. In that instant, just as he reached the top, he was
> struck by a direct flak burst and disappeared in a flash of light.
> Only pieces remained and they fluttered down toward the green-
> brown checkerboard earth, glinting in the sunlight as they fell.
> There was some yelling and scrambling around as we awaited
> more flak, but our gunners had already been dumping what
> chaff they had left from the bomb runs and the puffs chased the
> foil strips down and behind us. The firing had come either from
> barges or railroad flatcars moved in to cover the often used route
> we had flown, and would be withdrawn and moved again in time
> (1992, p. 117).

Horrific as the occasion is, it provides more than a reminder
that there are no such things as idle moments in war. At any time
death and destruction may intervene, as even crew members soak-
ing up the pleasures of a day off would realize once the V-1 flying
bomb offensive began in mid-1944. But the author of *Crewdog* sees
more to the lost Mustang than an interruptive irony, and with the
distance of memory can appreciate how the incident affects him to
this day. For just who was that young pilot who in a moment of supreme beauty could not resist showing off his fighter and was quite
literally consumed in the process, at the very height of his triumph
apotheosized into a flash of fire and pall of smoke?

"Perhaps at some time when he was a teen-aged kid," Matt
speculates, "he had come close to an airplane for the first time, on
some sunny afternoon, and reached out and touched it, and the
magic reached back and gripped him too and carried him to that
point over Holland on that day." Well read in the literature of air
combat, the author knows he's just described the beginning of so
many flyers' memoirs; early on in *Crewdog* he writes just such a
passage himself. But the lesson carries much further. "Sometimes,
even now," John Matt admits, "when I hear the name 'Mustang' I
think of this event, the first time I had seen an airplane shot down,
this first blood, and no matter what I am doing, a pang of regret
strikes my heart" (pp. 117-18).

And so not just the peaceful moments but a person's most
treasured and motivating memories are changed by the nature of
war, changed to become new beliefs that accompany one through
postwar life.

Chapter 4

Mediterranean Theater

BASED ON THE WAY flyers experienced it, the Mediterranean Theater of Operations (MTO) might have been part of a different war. Sometimes, especially near the end, objectives would be the same, and occasionally a squadron from the Fifteenth Air Force heading back south would see a formation from the Eighth turning west to England. But the planes themselves were different, with B-24 Liberators here, for the most part, as opposed to the Flying Fortresses that had been carrying the air war steadily eastward to Berlin. There were not as many Mustangs, either. Instead, aircrew from the Fifteenth would find themselves escorted by the twin-tailed P-38 Lightning, a plane held in some disfavor elsewhere. From Africa fighter missions were flown in P-40s, an aircraft otherwise consigned to the early doings of the American Volunteer Group—the Flying Tigers—in China and early action in the Pacific.

There was a different shape to this part of the war as well. Instead of flying from fixed bases to steadily advancing targets across Occupied France and Germany to the Nazi capital itself, the bomber force hammered away at the same objectives, yet from steadily advancing fields across Africa and into Italy. Because the enemy's land forces had to be cleared out of the way, fighters became tactical much earlier than from England and in a more consistent way, preparing not for one invasion (Normandy) but four (Sicily, Salerno, Anzio, and the south of France). Plus there was the matter of a special target, the oil refinery complex at Ploesti, which first drew B-24s into the Mediterranean Theater (when diverted from a planned transfer to China) in June 1942 and continued to swallow aircraft and men far into 1944. Three hundred thirty-nine Allied bombers would be lost here, more than at any other target during the war. The Eighth Air Force, of course, could point to its own initially terrible attrition over Schweinfurt, another so-called panacea target whose ball-bearing manufacture was said to be crucial to the German war effort. But hideous losses there were limited to the first two missions. Ploesti was hit repeatedly, no easier the last time than the first. Plus a tour in the MTO was fifty missions.

Flyers live on the ground, and crew and squadron life in Africa and then Italy was radically different from such life in England. Granted, there was much less fog and a great deal more sunshine. And compared to how the Cactus Air Force lived on Guadalcanal, there were other advantages as well. But with them came the biting, gritty sand of Africa, omnipresent between everything from human teeth to engine gears, while in Italy there was mud and a chilling damp that stretched from November through February on the less hospitable east coast where most Americans were based. There were no quaint, friendly villages where flyers could drink beer in pubs with the locals, no hedgerowed lanes for bicycle rides through lush countryside. Rougher and more sparse to begin with, southern Italy had been fought over by brutalizing armies, and what was once just a poor country was now laid desolate.

Above all there were few common customs and no shared language. Even more than missing the forty-eight-hour passes to London and rest-and-recuperation time in lovely English manor houses, flyers missed the feeling of being at least more than half at home. Even the happy squadron practice of adopting a bombed-out orphan was a different experience, more alien and discomforting because the child was less likely to be the round-cheeked, beaming Shirley Temple lookalike brought up amid fanfare from London than a starving, frightened castaway found huddling barefoot in the snow.

One wouldn't think that boarding a bomber or even walking across an airbase could be that different between England and Italy, but in memoir after memoir from the Fifteenth Air Force the pictures seem drawn from contrasting models. Perhaps it is the profile a B-24 presents, somewhat comical and lumbering, so that Luftwaffe pilots would call it a "furniture van" while its own aircrew came up with worse. In any event, the spectacle Leroy W. Newby presents in *Target Ploesti* (1983) is anything but heroic as the men gather before their somewhat silly looking airplane: "In full regalia, we didn't look so pretty either. With our flying suits, flying boots, parachute harnesses, and Mae Wests all in place, we felt as if we were in corsets. The most apt description of us was that we looked like a bunch of penguins waddling around. So if you can picture ten penguins trying to climb under a low fence, you have an idea of what we looked like as we struggled into our pregnant cow" (p. 22).

Granted, the low-slung Liberator with its tricycle gear is not the easiest craft to enter, but Newby extends his point to make the crewmen share the comedy of their plane's situation—all in an affectionate, nonjudgmental way. Indeed, those who fly from Africa and then Italy have to take a whimsical view of their appearance in order to keep spirits up. In *Bloody Skies* (1993) gunner Melvin W. McGuire can only laugh at his own appearance as he trundles out to check the bulletin board on a dreary Christmas Eve. "As it was bitterly cold," he notes, "I bundled up for the walk in sheepskin clothing—gunner's leather cap with sheepskin lining hanging over my ears, a muffler, two pairs of pants, and fur flying boots. I must have looked like a combination of a grizzly bear and Big Foot" (p. 359). The description reads as if from a comic strip—an intended effect, since it is only in this theater, observes Leroy Newby, that flyers find themselves "looking somewhat like Bill Mauldin's Willie and Joe" (1993, p. 110).

In a sense, the Mediterranean Theater becomes what the individual airmen make of it. From the sands of Africa to the mud of Italy, it is much more of a tabla rasa than the Eighth Air Force's Cambridgeshire and East Anglia. There, living quarters were in Nissen huts, unevenly heated but at least dry; if taking over a prewar RAF station, American officers might find themselves in fine accommodations indeed, and on a few occasions there was, in Battle of Britain tradition, the odd inn or even manor house to be requisitioned. In the Mediterranean, tents were the rule, on airbases set out upon the wastelands. How happy or miserable men would be depended on their ingenuity. On the first night a rainstorm hits Richard G. Byers's base in Libya, he and his crewmates learn the hard way that their tent has not been ditched to keep the water away; one of their first joint exercises in *Attack* (1984) is "to take everything off the ground stored under the cots and place all on our beds," with sleep "almost impossible" and "mud all over" (p. 21). By the time B-24 outfits get to Italy, their men are more adept at things, and little by little tents are made livable. Packing cases are knocked down and fashioned into wooden floors; oil drums are cut apart, filled with aviation fuel, and rigged to feed the flames of improvised heaters; there are even stories of enterprising crews trading base exchange items for heavy-duty building materials, transforming canvas quarters into houses and putting up officers' clubs as comfortable as anything the Eighth could offer. Yet other crews could care less. In *Those Who Fall* (1986) John Muirhead considers the difference:

> The tents, like houses in a village, varied in style and elegance. Some were models of good labor. They put up a brave front of secure comfort with wood floors made from bomb crates and crude furniture made from the same material. A few even had flowerpots hung from the doorframes to catch the light. But the plants didn't grow. Indifferent gardeners gave them little care, and the wisps of pale greenery struggled against the sunless days. There were other tents beyond redemption, erected in contempt of any acknowledgment of permanence. Their poles were awry; their lines slack and poorly pegged. They shuddered, flapping in the cold February winds, like the tattered pennants of desperate men (p. 5).

In the harsher realities of this theater contrasting attitudes play a larger role. A fifty-mission quota seems wildly unsurvivable; prominent targets, such as aircraft factories at Vienna and the refinery at Ploesti, are among the most heavily defended in Europe; and between them and home base are the Alps, a 15,000-foot hurdle that forces planes to fly so high that they show up early on German radar, not to mention proving impassable to disabled bombers on the way back. Among all this, could straightening a ridge pole or watering a flower make any real difference? "Our lives," John Muirhead explains, "were defined by a line from the present to a violent moment that must come for each of us. The missions we flew were the years we measured to that end, passing by no different from any man's except we became old and died soon" (p. 4).

Yet there are things that can be done to make a difference. A structuring element in Leroy Newby's *Target Ploesti* are notations of bombing scores. Mission by mission bomb-drop photos are studied and compared, with rankings posted for each squadron. When his own unit ranks first, the author reports it like coming out on top in the baseball standings. But close bomb patterns indicate more than just concentration over the target. Target formations were, in fact, not as tight as during the rest of the mission, when pilots (and not bombardiers sending adjustments to the automatic pilot during the target run) could keep their planes together for better defense. The measures of that defense are many, but all pertain to closely boxed formations. As such, there were no holes for attacking fighters to fly through. Moreover, any Messerschmitts or Focke-Wulfs that did venture close came within the massed firepower of a thirty-six-plane formation, each bomber positioned so that its thirteen guns would contribute to a virtual 100 percent coverage of the field. To even a Luftwaffe ace, messing with this would be like trying to pick up a mad porcupine. The better and more experienced an enemy fighter pilot was, the more likely he would stay away from tightly flown formations. Just like the weakly strung and poorly tended tents back at base, there were plenty of ragged squadrons ripe for attack.

Looking for the weak ones fit right into local strategy. On its missions north the Fifteenth Air Force would encounter fighters of the Seventh Air Division, the Luftwaffe's southern Germany defense unit commanded from Munich by Maj. Gen. Joachim Huth. Huth followed Adolf Galland's teaching that resources were used best when applied against specific squadrons in a bomber stream. There could be nothing more demoralizing, even terrorizing, than wiping out an entire unit—knocking a hole, as it were, in the group's base. This tactic fit perfectly with the relative weakness displayed by poorly flown squadrons, squadrons staffed by fatalists who'd surrendered to what they felt was statistical inevitability. But even if all squadrons in the stream were tightly formed, wiliness could overcome their discipline at times, such as when a staffel of Messerschmitts grouped themselves in an American-style formation and approached just when pilots and gunners were expecting their escort to join. Here a moment's relaxation could be fatal, opening up just the hole a fighter needed to pass through, diluting the field of fire sufficiently for the flashing Messerschmitt or Focke-Wulf to emerge unscathed.

Good bomber crews didn't let this happen. Flyers such as Leroy Newby and Melvin McGuire often describe fighters approaching and then turning away, looking for easier pickings elsewhere. With such reconfirmation, good crews become even better, seeing how the hard work of flying tightly and watching out from all stations pays off. Some of them have an edge. McGuire, for example, knows not just that he has been among the highest scoring gunners in his class, but that his fellows have each been among the most highly ranked pilots, navigators, bombardiers, flight engineers, and so forth. There's a method to this, as Air Force management assembles such high-scoring trainees into picked crews it hopes will develop into group leaders. But any crew that works well together stands a better chance; German fighter pilots seem to spot them a mile away, turning off for easier victims downstream. And so natural selection works its way toward providing crews that can fly their seemingly impossible fifty-mission tours, come back, and with the same talents for living in civilian life prosper into healthy old age from whence they can write their memoirs.

Which is one very practical reasons crews kept flying with each other, doing anything to avoid being broken up or even taken out of sequence on the countdown toward tour completed. Halfway through *Bloody Skies* Melvin McGuire has lost his initial optimism, seeing far too many casualties and having enough close calls himself that his attitude now borders on fatalism. But one element keeps him short of despair, and that's the knowledge that together his crew can do better than apart:

> All of us were flying sick, and we weren't supposed to fly in this condition. I flew with burned hands and bad head colds. Chambers finished his tour flying with one arm and a hand in a cast. We had a horror of not being able to fly with our crew. None of us wanted to miss a flight and have some knucklehead replacement joining the crew and doing something to cause the plane to get shot down. Also, nobody wanted to get behind the rest of the crew in the number of missions flown. Nobody wanted to finish his tour with another crew. We were a close, tightly knit crew. We were comfortable with one another and went to great lengths to help each other. We were a family (1993, p. 314).

Even a few days of R & R in Rome prove distracting, the author's attention drawn to the sound of aircraft engines above. "First I heard the Pratt-Whitneys, followed by the Wright Cyclones, and knew they had to be the Fifth Wing," McGuire notes as he emerges from a building. "Then my conscience began bothering me. I started worrying about the guys and wanted to get back up there. I felt I was gold bricking while they were still working" (p. 326).

Everyone wants to finish, and most want to finish together. But few crews can escape combat fatigue, which for several reasons seems to strike harder in Italy than in England. There's the fifty mission tour—double what the Eighth Air Force initially flew, at first justified by the number of closer, almost tactical assignments within Italy itself, but soon questioned when both air forces began bombing common targets such as the Messerschmitt factory at Regensburg; a tardy half-solution was devised to give double credit for such flights. Then come the psychological differences of fighting from Italy rather than from England. Not only were conditions more comfortable and the culture more accessible in the United Kingdom, but there the flyers of the Eighth Air Force were striking back at an enemy who had bombed their hosts. Everybody was on the same side, and the American bomber boys were doing something to right wrongs and settle scores. Italy, too, had been bombed, particularly the Foggia Plain from which the Fifteenth Air Force now operated. But the bombers had been Americans, hammering at the Germans who not only occupied the country but had used Foggia for their own main Luftwaffe base in opposing the Allied thrust from North Africa. The devastation McGuire and Newby and the others experience was one they had created themselves; the unhoused, sallow victims they lived among could scarcely see them as heroes. And think how hard it is to fight a war when being considered the goat.

These are reasons why crews finishing up in the Mediterranean seem even more tired than their counterparts from the ETO. Yet even returning airmen from the Eighth present a sobering spectacle to fresh crews on their way to Italy. Bombardier J. W. Smallwood writes about just such an encounter in *Tomlin's Crew* (1992). His pilots, navigator, and himself are sitting in the officers' club at Dakar, happy with their Atlantic crossing and speculating about what their combat life will be like. At this point Tomlin notices four other flyers, obviously the commissioned members of a crew themselves, but distinguished by "the look of veterans" and a manner "of casual indifference" (p. 86). When these others approach the bar, the rookie copilot joins them, but returns almost at once. "The one I spoke to wasn't looking for company," he reports. "I think they want to be alone." So much for hearing about the real thing. Later on the veterans sing a drinking song, but oddly subdued and off-key, after which they lapse into a profound silence, "all sitting, with hands on the table, faces cast down, staring at the table top." Smallwood himself is discomforted. "It was an eerie feeling," he recalls, "and I wanted to leave." That they do, but with the worry that these veterans seem tired beyond mere exhaustion. "Was there a weariness in those voices, something far away?" Smallwood wonders. "Any crew that could complete 25 missions out of England in that early stage of the war, with little fighter support against the Germans, must have been extraordinarily lucky, or skillful, or both. They should have had some pretty hairy tales to tell" (p. 87). But it's obvious that nerves and composure have passed the limits of testimony; Tomlin's crew will have to find out for itself.

What crew members learn can be quite shocking right from the start. Arriving at Tortorella, Smallwood hears that his is one of several new crews—replacements for a squadron that has suffered some heavy losses. The cot he's given is not a new one, making him wonder who has slept there before. The arrival at Amendola of McGuire's crew is even more discomforting, for they land in their brand new B-17 just as news arrives that the resident squadron has been wiped out, every single plane being shot down on a dangerous mission over Czechoslovakia. A tough-as-nails line chief, a regular army veteran of the USAAC, is crying; ground crews are inconsolable; a sober operations officer directs them to their tent, where unpacking has to be done amid the personal effects—wallets, rings, keepsakes—customarily left on pillows for retrieval after missions. Only this time retrieval will be done by quiet professionals of the Graves Registration Unit:

> They spread six white sheets outside the tent, one for each bunk, and started packing the personal effects in them. While they were packing, they asked us to go through the gear and remove anything their families shouldn't see—classified material, escape material, or anything of a personal nature that might embarrass their families. They carried a list and checked it against the effects which had been left. We were impressed with their efficiency. I went outside when they had finished packing the sheets, and, while they were wrapping up the sheets, I looked at the tents in the area. It was scary. Every tent had six bundles in front of it, filled with personal effects. Everywhere I looked, there were those bundles (p. 87).

Flying missions of their own, new crews go through a timely process. At first the novelty of combat carries them past the recognition of true danger; they find it hard to believe that flak and fighters are trying to kill *them*, and are able to remain relatively detached from the spectacle of other planes getting it, simply because they're others, not themselves. But then a plane nearby gets hit and disintegrates almost within reach. Or perhaps a close friend in another ship is severely wounded or killed. But there is still the insularity of self. Even when Melvin McGuire picks up a piece of flak in his vest, he can play with it as a toy and joke about the fact that had it struck just an inch or two away it might have slit his throat.

Lucky crews can fly entire tours without being wounded. But despite that, matters change. About one-third into their quota of missions—after five or six weeks of flying, approximately—memoirists begin showing signs of strain. In Richard Byers' *Attack*, recorded faithfully as a diary and reproduced with no apparent editing, the difficulties manifest themselves at 100 hours into his 300-hour tour (as measured from bases in North Africa earlier in 1943). Mission scrubs are detested as something worse to sweat out than an active sortie itself; turnbacks from target, because of weather or mechanical problems, are even more frustrating, for this ten hours of flying now won't count, even though almost all the risks have been the same. Milk runs, where there is no evidence of flak or fighters, become cherished. Worst of all, talk about malingering begins to surface: playing sick to skip a mission, or even shooting oneself in the foot to be sent home. Byers hears all of this and understands, for he's begun feeling terrible himself. And all without any real trouble or even close calls.

For Melvin McGuire, it is at about this same point that flak starts bothering him, not just during flight but in his nightmares. Over Germany he can rationalize it, appreciating how "The worst part was sitting there and taking that awful pounding and knowing there was nothing you could do." Unlike shooting at fighters, there's no way to oppose it, particularly on the fifty miles of a bomb run when the plane could not deviate, just when flak was worst. Elsewhere, sports metaphors have fueled the combat spirit, but here they work to confound it, "It was like being in a boxing match," the author of *Bloody Skies* complains, "where you were not allowed to hit back" (1993, p. 156).

The bombing war is clearly one of attrition. But attrition consumes more than shot-down planes and missing men. The toughest measure is taken of those who would otherwise survive, but who are being stressed to the point of ineffectiveness simply by the ongoing nature of the task. As many veterans have stated, the true measure of heroism was not getting in a plane and taking off to meet the enemy. That, on a one-time basis, could be done by almost anybody, and the enthusiasm of fresh crews shows that flak itself, as first encountered, might inspire no great fear. But to face it twenty-five, thirty-five, or ultimately fifty times was proof of real courage, courage that had the stamina to go at it repeatedly. "Our most harrowing thought," McGuire admits, "was that, once again, we were going to have to run that gauntlet for the next twenty-five or fifty miles. You prayed to come out alive on the other side of that living hell. This is what wore you down. You couldn't fight back. You could only sit and take it" (p. 157).

And so come what various memoirists call "the dreads," "the hoo-dooes," "the willies," "the chills," and so forth. More flyers accept the proferred shot of postmission whiskey, even two or four or five if others don't want it. Nonsmokers start to smoke. Cheerful guys turn grim, and optimists turn into worriers. Pilots, bombardiers, and gunners feel at the end of their string, even as the string of remaining missions stretches far ahead. "Combat fatigue" is the proper term for this state, and flight surgeons were sharp-eyed to spot it, for a crew member flying in such condition could be a menace to his plane. At such stages of exhaustion, rest was prescribed—perhaps a week in an R & R facility appropriately called a flak house. Why so? Because no matter what the specific cause of nervous depletion, flyers themselves preferred to call it being "flak happy." Leroy Newby finds amusement in what his squadron mates call "green flak"; his *Into the Guns of Ploesti* (1991) makes much of this coloring, said to be a sure sign of a flyer well past the limits of fatigue. Why is "seeing green flak" such a telling indication? Not just because there is none, but because flak is the worst enemy and its coloration can be crucial. If you see black flak, you're OK—it has burst far enough away not to harm you. Orange flak means trouble, for the burst is close by. Red flak means trouble, too: at the end of their firing program gunners would detonate a red shell to let German fighters know it was safe to make attacks. But green flak? No such thing, which indicates hallucinations.

Yet so many are the dangers from flak that rational comtemplations of it fill these books as well. B-24 navigator Donald R. Currier writes about it in *50 Mission Crush* (1992), how "sometimes we could pick out flak batteries on the ground firing at us." At 20,000 feet, it would take almost twenty seconds for an 88-mm shell to reach altitude. "I'd wonder," Currier recounts with no small amazement, "if I were looking at the shell being fired that was going to get us" (p. 131). There are other ways, too, that a bomber crew can feel like sitting ducks. Opposable as they are, Luftwaffe fighters have many ways of getting at them, all of which can be visibly measured. Machine-gun fire carries tracers; cannon ammunition is heavy enough that writer after writer customarily refers to such shells as being "lobbed" at them; later in the war fighters and converted light bombers carried rockets, with projectiles that approach the tail gunner's position looking like spiraling footballs. The cumulative effect of all these threats is the greatest. "Seems a person gets more concerned with survival," it occurs to Richard Byers when his tour is two-thirds done, "the more combat hours one acquires" (1984, pp. 200-201).

A curious fatalism pervades Fifteenth Air Force memoirs, particularly those from the bomber groups. From England, crews see missions as battling their way through, especially to a target that can be personified as Hitler or Goering. From Africa and Italy the objectives are strategically real but personally abstract, such as production capacity at Ploesti or worker morale at the Focke-Wulf plant outside Wiener-Neustadt. That the latter targets are defined with massed firepower second only to Berlin makes it all the more grim. Watching an escort of P-38s tangle with some pursuing Messerschmitts is just a diversion for John Muirhead in *Those Who Fall*. No movie action here, such as John Comer and Harry Crosby described in their respective Eighth Air Force narratives—rather just a picture of stolid dedication. "The bomber formation pressed on, indifferent to the melee: the slow, sullen progress never faltered, never changed; it moved with a purpose beyond understanding." The formation itself seems his objective, Muirhead believes: "A wide vapor trail lay behind us, a defiant pennant without valor proclaiming stubborn, plodding persistence, nothing else. The strike would be made. No matter what it cost, the strike would be made" (1986, p. 106). Redemption lies not in making the strike but somehow being out of it. "Every time I saw [the fighters]," the author notes, "I felt the same yearning to be as free as they were, to move as they did in soft, curling patterns above the bombers, or to roll away in a flash of motion as though abandoned to some impulse of delight." Even the language to describe fighters is so much lighter. "The sky was more a playground for them than a battlefield, or so it seemed to me," Muirhead allows. "I knew they fell and died as we did, but theirs must have been a brighter heaven" (p. 135). No wonder Leroy Newby's *Into the Guns of Ploesti* celebrates the occasion of a Liberator pilot finding a disabled bomber under attack and "roaring down from out of the sun, fighter style," to take on the offending Me-109. "The fighter pilot never knew what hit him as the steep-diving B-24 poured sixty-nine rounds per second for several seconds into the hapless Messerschmitt." Getting out of the stream and into the realm of more immediately purposeful action is a delight. "It was man bites dog," Newby appreciates, as "the Me-109 burst into flames and plummeted to earth, to the applause of a happy bomber crew" (1991, pp. 159-60).

Most Luftwaffe attackers must be dealt with from more confining circumstances. "Leading them with my gun was like trying to catch a weasel," complains Melvin McGuire. Their diving attack from high in the front brings them past the bombers at fantastic speeds, 500 mph or more, allowing for the bomber's forward progress. The Focke-Wulfs are in McGuire's case curving as well, moving them through three dimensions, as if to tie the gunners in knots. A New Mexican, McGuire finds another metaphor to capture the dynamism of this event: "They still reminded me of *banderilleros*, running toward a bull at an angle, and then sticking in the blade before twirl-

ing out of his way" (1993, p. 143). Fighters twirl, curve, and angle off
into the multiple dimensions of space; it is the huge but clumsy
bomber that lumbers on, consigned like the punch-drunk boxer or
harried bull to just take it and continue as far as possible. As in a
bullfight, the coup de grace won't come until later, much like the
technical knockout that's called after successive heaps of punishment become too much. This is the accumulation that wears one
down even before it takes one out.

It is at Ploesti that the most bombers go down in a flash. Leroy
Newby's second book, *Into the Guns of Ploesti*, builds on his first
study with accounts of the most spectacular action. Even practicing
for the early low-level mission is dangerous, where memories are
laced with humor to mask the fear of what looms ahead. "During
one of the low-level practice runs on 'Ploesti,'" a model of the refinery complex built in the Libyan desert near Bengasi, "one of the
bombers was forced onto the ground by a plane above it. The plane
skidded for 200 yards on the ground, engines still operating." This
is just the fate crews have been fearing, but in practice at least
there is room for a miracle to be pulled off. Skidding through the
desert at almost 200 mph gets everyone's attention, Newby agrees.
"Then the desperate pilot gave the engines full throttle and lifted his
bomber back off the ground. That evening the pilot was given an
award for the all-time distance record for taxiing with the wheels
up" (1991, p. 24). On the celebrated low-level raid of 1 August 1943
itself, where a navigational error sent the lead force into Ploesti
from the wrong direction (and through its most lethal defenses),
Newby again looks for the wryly unusual—not just bombers bursting into flame, but coming through the inferno in marvelous ways.
Note what happens when part of a fractured group turns south
over the city:

> This particular deviation from the original plan resulted in an in-
> congruous scene: low-flying bombers roaming the streets of
> Ploesti; civilians on the sidewalks waving to the air crews as ma-
> chine gunners on rooftops were firing at the flyers. The aerial
> gunners, forbidden from firing their guns over the city, could
> only wave back. A gunner on the odyssey observed they had run
> ten red lights on one street (p. 57).

But when planes go down, they do so in spectacular ways, too. One
particularly hideous sight is that of "a bomber striking a barrage
balloon cable and climbing up the cable until it hit a contact bomb.
The explosion blew the entire wing off the plane" (p. 75).

Newby's characterization of the Ploesti experience is an apt one: that of young flyers "sending their souls through the Invisible," as paraphrased from Edward FitzGerald's *Rubáiyát of Omar Khayyám.* This was the third heaviest defended target in Europe, after Berlin and Vienna; but its concentration of flak guns was the thickest, and raids were scheduled to allow maximum preparation time for fighters, flak gunners, and the laying down of smoke screens. The 120-mile run-in to Vienna, with antiaircraft fire all the way, was indeed a gauntlet. But Ploesti was a cauldron boiling with all the elements capable of bringing bombers to catastrophe. For B-24s, everything was against them: their propensity to catch fire, their difficulty in maintaining tight formations, and their inability to take as much punishment as B-17s. Fortresses could make it back from a target on two engines; thanks to their modern airfoil needing higher flight speeds, Liberators were marginal on three.

No wonder Philip Ardery marvels at the hellish scene he must take his plane through. In *Bomber Pilot* he pegs his altitude at just above the refinery's smokestacks. Previous waves have already dropped their bombs, with delayed-action fuses meant to keep the way clear. But things are blowing up everywhere, thanks to explosions among oil tanks and cracking equipment on the ground:

> We found ourselves at that moment running a gauntlet of tracers and cannon fire of all types that made me despair of ever covering those last few hundred yards to the point where we could let the bombs go. The antiaircraft defenses were literally throwing up a curtain of steel. From the target grew the column of flames, smoke, and explosions, and we were headed straight into it.
>
> Suddenly Sergeant Wells, our small, childlike radio operator who was in the waist compartment for the moment with a camera, called out, "Lieutenant Hughes' ship is leaking gas. He's been hit hard in his left wing fuel section."
>
> I had noticed it just about that moment. I was tired of looking out the front at those German guns firing at us. I looked out to the right for a moment and saw a sheet of raw gasoline trailing Pete's left wing. He stuck right in formation with us. He must have known he was hard hit because the gas was coming out in such volume that it blinded the waist gunners in his ship from our view. Poor Pete! Fine religious, conscientious boy with a young wife waiting for him back in Texas. He was holding his ship in formation to drop his bombs on the target, knowing if he didn't pull up he would have to fly through a solid room of fire with a tremendous stream of gasoline gushing from his ship. I flicked the switch intermittently to fire the remote-control, fixed fifty caliber machine gun specially installed for my use. I watched my tracers dig

the ground. Poor Pete. How I wished he'd pull up a few hundred feet and drop from a higher altitude (1978, pp. 104-5).

At this point Ardery experiences the rite of passage Newby's books describe, sending his soul through the invisible. Not only is the other side as yet unimaginable, but the barrier itself seems impassable. In fact, what lies beyond cannot be pictured because an obstacle has done much more than obscure the present: it has blotted out all effective manner of dealing with the future. When that is allowed to happen, individuals stop living, long before any actual death. In the Fifteenth Air Force, it is evidenced by pilots who fly loose formations, gunners who become lax at their positions, and crews in general who let everything go to seed just because the odds aren't in their favor.

What does Ardery do? He prays, a bit fatalistically because "I didn't think I could come out alive," going "into the furnace" as he is. Yet if he has any doubts about his own survival, there are none whatsoever about Pete Hughes's, for Pete's plane is entering the inferno awash with raw gasoline.

With this thought Ardery dives in and everything goes black with smoke. Beneath him a boiler house explodes and the B-24 is knocked tail high. "We must have cleared the chimneys by inches," Ardery guesses, and then as the smoke clears must struggle to avoid clipping house tops. "We were through the impenetrable wall," he discovers, "but what of Pete? I looked out right. Still he was there in close formation, but he was on fire all around his left wing where it joined the fuselage" (p. 105).

Here is where Philip Ardery feels himself about to cry. His friend has survived the impossible, laying bombs squarely on target in the process. But now he must fight to save himself and his men. That means dropping speed by half (from 210 mph to less than 110) and finding clear ground on which to belly in, both before exploding. Problems with airspeed and fire, of course, are the B-24's two greatest weaknesses, and so once again survival should be ruled out. Yet as before the pilot remains resolute:

> Wells, in our waist gun compartment, was taking pictures of the gruesome spectacle. Slowly the ship on our right lost speed and began to settle in a glide that looked like it might come to a reasonably good crash-landing. But flames were spreading furiously all over the left side of the ship. I could see it plainly, as it was on my side. Now it would touch down—but just before it did, the left wing came off. The flames had been too much and had literally burnt the wing off. The heavy ship cartwheeled and a great

flower of flame and smoke appeared just ahead of the point where last we had seen a bomber. Pete had given his life and the lives of his crew to carry out his assigned task. To the very end he gave the battle every ounce he had (pp. 105-6).

Thus is passage attained: for Hughes to a heroic death, for Ardery to a future that encompasses finishing the war and, after a long and successful postwar career in law, writing this book. In witnessing the spectacle, he undergoes the passage himself, but only in writing does it assume useful meaning. Consider the last two sentences. By themselves, they could have been spoken by anyone, and in their verbal nature actually have the airy quality of political and moralistic speech. But what precedes them shows the work of imagination and intelligence, the product not only of eyes observing fact but also of a mind working on them to give substance and importance. The hoped for peace of seeing the plane "settle" and then "glide" is countered by the hellish flames, which spread, burn through, and eventually do their work of taking the wing off—just before touchdown, the moment when Pete would be safe. After flame comes smoke, naturally enough; but here it is a finalizing smoke that shapes itself into a commemorative, funereal "flower" where the plane had last appeared. With these images in mind—and especially after Ardery's careful description of his and the other plane's actual passage through the invisible—the last two lines have much more meaning.

Such rites of passage, and the passages witnesses write about them, transform the horrors of the air war into something better for the crews that fight it. But what Ardery describes is a common tactic, that of pushing on to the objective regardless of enemy pressure. And the success of this tactic becomes an important part of the bomber offensive's overall strategy. The circumstance Ardery describes is not unique; from their positions in formation, pilots and other crew members admire severely disabled planes that nevertheless go onto the target, knowing that completing the bomb run surely seals their fates. In *Bloody Skies* Melvin McGuire's waist gun position provides a good perspective on another act of courage, in this case an attack on Munich where the heavy concentration of flak guns has "turned the day into night," creating one more obstacle such as Newby and Ardery have described. Having passed through himself, McGuire looks back from the rally point to see a lone B-17 on the other side. "It had a couple of engines on fire, but was flying straight and level into the target, not wavering one bit as flak burst all around it. It continued into and over the target, all by itself." This is especcially daunting, the author knows, because "At times it was completely obscured by flak; it looked like every flak battery around Munich was firing at it." Almost completely on fire for the last two miles of its run-in to the target, the Fortress just has time to make its drop before going down. No parachutes are observed.

"I never saw this plane's number or squadron markings, never knew any of the names of the crew," McGuire regrets, "but that B-17 epitomized what we were all about. While with the Second Bomb Group, I never once personally observed a single bomber in our squadron or group turning back from a target because of enemy opposition or pressure" (1993, p. 345). In fact, no American plane in any theater of operation ever did abort for such reasons. Weather problems might ground a mission; technical malfunctions might send the odd aircraft back to base. But never did German flak or fighters stop an American attack. Just knowing this made crews eager not to break the record, and also confident that opposition alone was no reason to turn back. Precisely the opposite effect thus worked its magic on the Germans. No matter what they did, no matter how many flak guns were pulled back from the Eastern front (where they had good use as antitank weapons), no matter how much of the Luftwaffe's resources were put into air defense of the Reich, those formations of B-17s and 24s would never stop. A better deterrent against German morale could hardly be imagined, part of the same wisdom characteristic of the fighter squadrons who were taught never to break away from an oncoming Focke-Wulf or Messerschmitt, lest word spread among the Luftwaffe that their opponents could be thus overcome.

Here is the true other side to Leroy Newby's daunting prospect of sending one's soul through the invisible. He notes it himself on his first mission to Ploesti, which because it is the Air Force's fourteenth raid on the great refinery complex promises the chance of survival and success. Others have gone before and returned; no attack has ever been turned back. He jokes about the "one advantage" his crew has over the first low-level raiders: "we had certainly heard of the place" (1983, p. 56). But Newby has also heard plenty of stories and knows the test can be passed, that the passage can indeed be made. This allows him the confidence to hold securely to his belief in the future, knowing that useful lessons from the past have been confirmed. Most of all, it lets him function well in the present, rather than succumbing to the fatalism that weakened other crews to the point of becoming their own worst enemies. A sense of rightness overtakes him on his first mission to the dread target, as recorded in *Target Ploesti*: "While flying high above the clouds, I found the sight from my side window so dramatic, I forgot about Ploesti for a few moments. I was struck by the contradiction of the beauty of 500 four-engine bombers in orderly formation, a thousand contrails streaming behind, forming a spectacular skyscape on a peaceful morning, with the purpose soon to be revealed" (1983, p. 57).

As happens, Newby already knows the purpose and meaning behind it. Ploesti, devilish cauldron that it is, is wrong. His bomber formation, meant to take it out of existence, is right. Thus fortified, the bomber crewman can proceed. In *Those Who Fall*, the initially skeptical John Muirhead comes to feel the same way, looking at a similar sight and finding himself overcome not by terror but by "peace and contentment." The flak forgotten, he lets "Our small armada" fill him with pride as he looks at each of his group's four squadrons and is "awed by their steadfast symmetry. I was one of them. I would never be in better company" (1986, p. 142).

Fighter warfare in the Mediterranean presents its own challenges. Action there began in response to Rommel's Afrika Corps and its objective of capturing the Suez Canal, an act that would have strangled Allied supply lines from the south and made the Axis dominant in this theater. Hence this region was chosen for the first sustained invasion of enemy-held territory. On 8 November 1942, American air and naval forces began a successful assault on Morocco, taking over weakly defended Vichy French installations in the region of Casablanca. Soon U.S. fighter wings became active farther east across the desert, providing support for the British Army striving to push Rommel back into Tunisia. Then, with the Afrika Corps' collapse imminent, the Ninth Air Force began its bomber offensive from Libya, later to be absorbed into the Fifteenth and moved to Italy.

For fighters especially, the African and Italian campaigns were ones of transition. Once in full swing, it meant being almost always on the move, the A flight of a squadron pushing ahead as an advanced ground party to set up a new base while B flight continued to fly, for the moment, from the group's previously secured field—a situation far less common in the European Theater, where the Fourth Fighter Group's permanent bases in England remained within range of the advancing line right to the war's end. And so in all aspects, from launching its assault aboard carriers through taking orders from the British to hopscotching its way up the mainland of

Italy, fighter warfare in the MTO was conducted in much different dimensions.

Those dimensions are most radically different at the start, when planes otherwise typecast for the Pacific—Grumman Wildcat fighters, Douglas Dauntless dive bombers—make their appearances over Casablanca. Two navy lieutenants, M.T. Wordell and E.N. Seiler, write about it in *"Wildcats" Over Casablanca* (1943), a self-styled "fly on the wall" type narrative (p. ix) in which the observer is allowed to see and hear everything without being observed himself. In the tradition of *Skyways to Berlin* published in the same year, it rallies homefront morale and presents its aviators in sympathetic postures. But unlike its companion volume, there is no need to characterize the protagonists as victims, for fighters are by nature a defensive weapon—even here in a seaborne assault, where their role is to secure air cover for troops coming aground.

That they do, in admirable fashion. Less attention is given to the work of the Dauntlesses, those "veritable tanks of the air" who pit themselves against "the crawling armor of the land troops" (p. 127). Nor is there much about the seaborne assault, either. Instead, Wordell and Seiler keep their fly-on-the-wall eyes trained on the Grumman Wildcats, the dashing Red Rippers whose wild-boar escutcheon represents their vigor in the air. That their convoy is such that "nothing had ever been seen like this since the days of the Spanish Armada" (p. 8) and that in contemporary terms it covers an area "equal to that of the state of Rhode Island" (p. 25) is only graspable when seen from the air, from these same Grummans out on patrol. In this and in many other ways, the authors are more accurately a fly in the sky than on a wall.

Thus the first dramatic scene from fighter warfare in the MTO is that of these Wildcats getting aloft from their carrier. Mounting the flight deck as dawn breaks "is like a scene from a movie," replete with silhouettes emerging from shadows to dance around planes while the dark shape of the carrier's superstructure is profiled against the gathering light. "You are conscious of the black etched lines of the bridge of the foretruck," a pilot is quoted, "and of the battle flags whipping in the wind. In the dawn light, everything looks much bigger than it actually is." Lined up for instructions from the flight-deck officer, this same pilot describes what happens next, a scene common from the Pacific but unique in this part of the war:

> He stands next to the island braced against the wind. He points
> to you with his left hand, wags his forefinger at you quickly to

make you open up to full throttle as you test your oil and fuel pressures and check your magnetos. "Everything O.K.?" "Right," you nod at him. He looks ahead to check the interval of the last plane that took off, holds his flag up and then quickly drops it. As you release the brakes, the plane leaps forward, its tail swishing to and fro as you adjust the rudder to take care of the increased torque. For a while the tail seems to dance, rather like a ballet dancer, and then settles as you get speed—more and more speed. You approach the bow, and the plane begins to feel lighter and lighter, becoming buoyant, and suddenly you are away from the frantic noise of the flight deck and alone in the humming silence of your own plane. It is the most terrific change of atmosphere a human can experience—as if an express train suddenly passed you, standing on the platform of a local station, leaving silence—vibrant, electric, but almost peaceful (p. 50).

But then even air combat in this operation involves different factors. Because their adversaries are French, it is hard to have a bloodthirsty attitude—on either side. Courtesies and gallantry prevail; disabled planes are waved off rather than finished to the death, and the few American aviators who are captured find themselves treated with friendliness and even camaraderie. The whole idea of opposition seems preposterous, not just when Grumman Wildcats dogfight with other American planes (Curtiss P-40s sold to the French in 1939) but especially when French outfits being engaged are identified as the Escadrille Lafayette and Capt. Eddie Rickenbacker's old Hat-in-the-Ring Squadron.

Throughout the Mediterranean campaign North Africa remains a strange, even storybook land. Later on in the war, bomber crews en route to Italy or England find their layovers there the most exotic part of the long haul that has included stops in the West Indies, Brazil, and Senegal. Forbidden cities, the casbah, natives whose life-styles seem more than a world removed from their own—all make for a strange interlude between training in the United States and battling with the Luftwaffe. In *Mustang Ace* (1991) Robert J. Goebel profits from being told the nature of the rear-area central facility at Telergma, Algeria, where he spends some time before heading on to Naples and his first base at Castel Volturno. Not so fortunate is Melvin McGuire, who in *Bloody Skies* fears he is undergoing a paranormal experience when landing there:

Chills went over my body after my first glimpse of the outpost. I had definitely seen this fort before. Climbing out of the truck, I knew the location of all the facilities. Everything—headquarters, the barracks, the kitchen facilities, the gate, the well, even the palm trees—looked familiar. As we walked around the old post, everything was exactly where I knew it would be. It was an eerie feeling. I was beginning to believe in reincarnation by the time we returned to our quarters (1993, pp. 74-75).

Goebel, however, is forewarned and thus forearmed. "The permanent installation at FTC looked like a movie set from *Beau Geste*," he reports. "In fact, the site *had* been a French Foreign Legion outpost" where the famous movie was filmed (1991, p. 62). McGuire spends an uneasy night there before he's told the fact, which puts everything in order. "I must have seen that movie five or six times," he admits, "so no wonder everything looked familiar" (1983, p. 75).

The fighter war in Africa is atypical from what was being fought by the Fourth Fighter Group and others based in England. Pushing Rommel's tank corps back into Tunisia and eventually out of Africa made it a tactical affair. Not only were American squadrons taking orders from the British, but some were flying Spitfires—a plane Bob Goebel loved and at first regretted having to exchange for a Mustang. Then came strikes across the Mediterranean, once more against ground targets, giving poor-performance altitude fighters such as the P-40 and P-38 a chance to redeem themselves. Interestingly, the two principal memoirs of this fighter war in Africa treat other issues as well—issues of discrimination in life and alienation within the service. North Africa was the original combat station for Benjamin O. Davis, Jr.'s Ninety-ninth Pursuit Squadron, the first all-African-American outfit in the Army Air Force and a unique experiment in the eventual integration of this service arm; *Benjamin O. Davis, Jr.: An Autobiography* (1991) thus has two stories to tell. But so does Frederic Arnold's *Doorknob Five Two* (1984), where the issue is anti-Semitism endured by the author from a hostile member of his own squadron as well as feared from his potential captors on the ground. Arnold's story is doubly complicated by the fact that he has felt compelled to disguise his combat status from his parents, letting his seriously ill father believe he's merely training pilots from rear-area safety. Both books, then, see an already different nature of air combat in specially attuned ways. Hence when either author succeeds, the victory is a double one and more, relating to much larger issues in the war itself and also in the nature of postwar life.

Because Frederic Arnold's war has such personal dimensions, his narrative often focuses on the individual. He is stunned, for example, when his leader disappears off his wing, consumed in the orange and black flash of an exploding flak shell. In a moment, he's witnessing his first enemy kill, as a squadron mate disables a Messerschmitt by setting its engine aflame. "The canopy separated," Arnold observes, "and the German pilot stood up in the cockpit as if to reach for cool air." The description is precise, even intimate, as the young flyer notes just what his adversary is undergoing: "His torso, bent back under the force of the wind, stood in full view behind the blowtorch of his engine." This, however, is not all, for Arnold has yet to see the actual kill. When it happens, the event is as personal as a homicide, at least as the memoirist reports it. "Brooks fired again," he writes. "The upper half of the man, cut clean, tumbled past the tail and shot like a cannon ball over the top of Brooks' plane" (1984, p. 106). What happens next? The mild-mannered, sensitive, and sometimes persecuted pilot turns into a killer himself, sighting another Me-109 and finding himself screaming, "Kill the son-of-a-bitch!" A wing breaks off and the disintegrating plane cartwheels away, carrying its trapped pilot with it. "My God," Arnold realizes, "I've shot down a plane and killed a man," his first. Yet the picture of this event that he carries away corresponds to the original sight of his own leader's death: "He disappeared in seconds, just like Sadler." But then, when he overhears a grateful radio call from the bombers they're escorting, Arnold's attitude withdraws. "I slouched deep in my seat," he recalls, "my face buried in my mask. I didn't kill that man, I told myself. The squadron did" (p. 107).

Benjamin Davis also takes the war personally—as he must, for being in command of first the Ninety-ninth Pursuit Squadron and then the entire 332nd Fighter Group put responsibility squarely on his shoulders. How his men performed would influence not just tactics and strategies but how the Air Force would deal with racial integration. At the time this policy had highly placed opponents; it is distressing to read the names of generals widely praised for their other work—such as Monk Hunter and William Momyer—making arguments against Davis's units that had no basis whatsoever except in racial prejudice. Granted, he can credit plenty of cooperation as well. "A strong bond exists among those who fly regardless of race" (1991, p. 97), and one of those bonds existed with the squadron that first helped them train in Africa, the Twenty-seventh. This was the outfit led by Col. Philip Cochran, a dashingly successful commander who was the model for Flip Corkin in the comic strip "Terry and the Pirates." Confident of their own abilities and inspired by Cochran's example, pilots of the Ninety-ninth took a major role in strafing missions against the island of Pantelleria off the coast of

Sicily, the first objective in military history to be conquered by air power alone.

But then came Colonel (later General) Momyer's critical report that "the Negro type has not the proper reflexes to make a first-class fighter pilot" (p. 103). Momyer's support for this thesis was the relatively low number of enemy planes shot down by Davis's flyers. The charge was a patently unfair one, Davis argued, because it ignored "the nature of most of the P-40 squadron missions—dive bombing and support of ground troops—during a period when encounters with enemy aircraft were practically nonexistent" (p. 107). Thus it was doubly important that the squadron did exceptionally well providing air cover for the Anzio invasion. Here, on two successive days in January 1944 Davis's pilots shot down German fighters as fast as they encountered them, eight on 27 January and four more on 28 January, all of them vaunted Focke-Wulf 190s. Planes damaged and those listed as probables brought the forty-eight-hour total to eighteen. This prompted a congratulatory message from Gen. Hap Arnold himself. After a visit in April Gen. Ira Eaker, the theater air commander, informed the Ninety-ninth Pursuit Squadron that it was regarded as the command's "most hardened and experienced P-40 unit" and the one earmarked for "pinpoint dive-bombing missions close to our frontline troops" (p. 119).

By the time Davis's group was reequipped with P-51 Mustangs, easily identifiable as "the Red Tails," they had become heroes to other units with whom they worked. Shot up badly over Regensburg with one engine feathered and another running poorly, Melvin McGuire's B-17 runs so short of fuel that his crew is certain they'll have to bail out. Just then the Red Tails make their appearance, not only protecting the bomber from being shot down but escorting it to a safe, virtually tanks-dry landing at their own base, where the bomber crew is given first-class hospitality. "That meal was just another example of the excellent outfit they were," McGuire writes in *Bloody Skies*. "The relationship between the Tuskegee Airmen and the bombers of the Fifteenth Air Force couldn't have been better. They were one of the premier groups in Europe." Unlike a few general officers with misconstrued notions of race and tradition, McGuire could see just what Davis's men delivered and was one to benefit mightily from it. "I can't say enough good about the Tuskegee Airmen," he emphasizes. "Their boast was that they never lost a bomber they were escorting, and I believe they were right" (1993, p. 302).

The fact that every other air group in the war is completely Cau-
casian throws relationships with the Ninety-ninth and the 332nd
into higher profile. It is odd that Davis's people were a worry to generals at desks back in Washington, D.C., while to lieutenants in the
cockpit and sergeants at the waist-gun position they were heroes. To
those who would object that today's memoirists are cautious in their
political correctness, portraying themselves as advocates of integration a generation before civil rights became more fashionable (and the
law), one only has to look at how writers like Leroy Newby and Frederic Arnold portray their experiences of the time. There's no fancy
styling here; instead, their narratives show young men from virtually
all-white backgrounds doing their best to meet and work with people
whose racial representatives are familiar to them mostly as stereo-
types. At the time, the African-Americans Leroy Newby would have
known best were Satchel Paige, Josh Gibson, Buck Leonard, and
other stars from the Negro National Baseball League who barn-
stormed through Newby's Pennsylvania neighborhood. Their play
was majestic. "Then, after the Grays or Crawfords had built up a
good lead over the local Church League All Star team," Newby recalls
in *Target Ploesti*, "they would start their comedy routines, with patter
and comments that broke up the crowd. It was always a fun evening,
especially when Paige would call in the outfield and infield, and then
strike out the side while the seven fielders sat around the mound."
Those memories come back when from his bombardier's position the
author can switch radio channels and listen to the same lively language games from his fighter escort. "Now we were being treated to
the same kind of carefree dialogue, but it wasn't a game" (1983,
p. 80). Overhearing the same kind of talk, Arnold's P-38 squadron
contrasts it with that of the British, whose own public school game
day patter and cries of "Tally Ho!" are equally distinctive. When the
Tuskegee Airmen are encountered on the ground, Arnold's narrative
becomes more serious, for one pilot in his squadron shames himself
with racist remarks—the same pilot who has been tormenting
Arnold for being Jewish.

    That issues of prejudice emerge in the Mediterranean Theater
may be coincidental, but they fit the general mood of the air war here
being treated less glamorously. The B-17 from England was the
iconic bomber, not the squat and sometimes troubled B-24; the Mustang was the flashy fighter, looking so much better in comparison to
the planes that flew from Africa and Italy, the P-40 and P-38. Top
journalists traveled first class, and such accommodations were

available, with all the trimmings, in London—certainly not in Bengasi or Foggia. Especially slighted in the news was the fighter pilot's role in ground attack, an increasingly important part of the Italian campaign as German supply lines from the north had to be cut and retreating forces kept disorganized. This meant railroads and bridges were prime targets, together with motorized equipment on the roads—none of it as attractive to journalists as shooting down Messerschmitts or flattening Berlin. In *World War II Fighter-Bomber Pilot* (1988), Bill Colgan understands how this type of combat does not fit the newspaper writer's formula of box scores, even when attacking airfields:

> A fighter-bomber pilot's war was not one of individual statistics and records on combat results. Those were tallied by mission, unit, and on up the line, growing into massive scores of varied targets destroyed and damaged by fighter-bombers on a theater-wide basis. Even so, many reports on fighter-bomber operations stressed only results in terms of the contribution made to the support of ground forces. For example, one report on the all-out effort we participated in on enemy airfields in April [1945] emphasized that the Seventh Army operated almost completely free of enemy air attacks in its push through Germany. Such examples regarding interdiction and direct support results were almost unlimited in number back through the war (p. 204).

Earlier, during the Anzio operation, Colgan had seen just how cold the journalistic shoulder could be. Back from his mission over the beachhead, he finds the debriefing tent so filled with reporters that there's hardly room to get in. Great interest is shown in stories about how many German planes were shot down. But as soon as the intelligence officer begins listing trucks and tanks, "the place cleared out as if something offensive had been said. I didn't see a note taken. Obviously the news people were not very interested in trucks and tanks" (p. 64). Yet Colgan's narrative shows how there are descriptive feasts aplenty in his style of warfare, such as what happens when his fighters escort a flight of light bombers being zeroed in on by 88-mm flak so efficiently that "it looked more like a blob of thick black smoke moving across the sky than a formation of airplanes" (p. 61). At such low levels the war is much more immediate, yet not the type of story journalists favor. Close observation was needed, something akin to an infantry correspondent—which, of course, the conditions of air combat did not allow.

And so descriptions are left to the memoirists, recalling forty years later just what it was like. For the invasion of southern

France, Colgan is up early, circling his airfield well before dawn while hundreds of aircraft assemble for takeoff beneath him:

> From the ground there were several unforgettable sights. First was the overall movement of airplane lights from every parking area on the field in a mass migration toward the runway. Then set after set of those lights went roaring into the night, one set right behind another, each set now augmented with blue-white exhaust glows. Those sets of lights gathered into four-ship missions and moved out in streams, joining more airplanes moving out in streams from other fields on Corsica, and in turn joining streams flowing overhead from Italy and possibly Sardinia (1988, p. 101).

Sets of planes and streams of light multiply and flow together just like Colgan's language, the same words accumulated for effect as they roll toward deliberate action. This is itself the effect he sees happening below. "Once into solid streams, one observer said there were simply too many lights too close together to think of them as individual airplanes—it all looked more like gigantic flows of lava moving across the sky" (p. 102). When daylight comes and the operation does its aggressive work, tearing apart almost everything military that's moving, Colgan can only wonder at the massive destruction. "I couldn't help thinking what a tremendous sight of war we were seeing there on the ground," he marvels. "I wondered if anyone other than God and we three pilots had ever seen anything like it" (p. 109).

The actual business of taking one's air war to the ground is very personal. Few pilots can say they enjoy strafing. For one reason it is more dangerous, about the most dangerous thing a fighter can do, where small flak or even a lucky rifle bullet can bring a plane down with no chance for escape. As for making kills, the classic fighter-jock attitude of those undertaking the war from England fails to transfer to the Mediterranean. In the more rarefied world of the Fourth and Fifty-sixth Fighter Groups, it was the machine rather than the person that was the target. In Italy, however, the roads were full of Germans; and while strafing missions across France might have been directed more toward locomotives and rolling stock, here the targets were quite recognizably individuals whose lives were on the line—and quite visibly in the line of fire. Consider the surprise Mark Savage feels in *Those Were the Days* (1993) when his squadron surprises a truck convoy heading north from Rome. "We counted almost thirty in the bunch," he recalls. "It was a picture perfect mission. We came over the hill and there they were, on the roll. A large cloud of dust marking their trail." Sweeping down for the kill is simple:

> On the first pass they never knew what hit them. About a third of them were left burning as we pulled up for the next pass. I came screaming down on this pass and hit three trucks. I watched in awe as the men seemed to just jump about 15 to 20 feet in the air. I looked again and realized that, *good God! these guys weren't jumping. It was my 50 caliber bullets that caused this.*
>
> Pulling up over-head, I decided that I had enough of this carnage. I watched the angels of death deal out their message and felt half-sick. It wasn't too long and it was over as fast as it started. A huge pall of smoke now hung over the valley as we started for home (p. 54).

The different dimensions of this Mediterranean air war and the fighting in it make for a more intimate style of description. Even escorting a bomber raid is different when the target is Ploesti, where Robert Goebel finds it "horrifying to watch the bombers disappear into that block of smoke" that characterized the massed defenses. "Occasionally, one would fall out of the bottom," he notes, "out of control—sometimes spinning, sometimes afire. We all watched for chutes, and someone would count them aloud on the R/T. 'There's three of them. There comes another. There's two more.' Long pause. 'I guess that's it'" (1991, p. 100). This same attentiveness carries over into his own war, where engaging German fighters is always a startling experience. "The sensation I felt at encountering an Me-109—of recognizing the rounded, blunt nose; the short wings, the long, thin fuselage; and small rounded tail—was like a stab in the chest," Goebel recalls, the sensation as fresh today as it was nearly fifty years ago. "The mottled camouflage paint, the large crosses, the greenhouse cockpit enclosure all screamed it out: 109!" Here are not rote details of aircraft recognition or even a customary spirit of "Tally-Ho!" Instead, the excitement is one of appreciating the danger for what it is. "With the realization came a rush of adrenaline," the author reports, "and my mind and body leaped to a new level of awareness and intensity. I know my pulse rate shot up, not from fear but from excitement and keenness" (p. 181).

With fewer stylizations of glory there are more opportunities to see the war for what it is. Rarely are mythological structures imposed upon it; rather, like Leroy Newby's characterization of the Ploesti experience as a passage of one's soul through the invisible, myths are created by the rigors of air combat rather than the other way around.

Preconceptions are factors, but become far less important than what's learned by careful attention to detail. The air war from England too was different from what preceded it—both World War I and even the Battle of Britain, which concluded just a month before the first Eagle squadron began operating on its own.

Above all, flyers in this theater resist the impositions of rhetoric. Not that they lacked rhetoric, and from genuine heroes, no less. General Jimmy Doolittle commanded these flyers. If anyone could claim legendary status, it was him. He had bombed Tokyo, leading a force of carrier-launched B-25s. Before that, when the young men of the Fifteenth Air Force were impressionable boys being romanced by flight, he had been a world-class air racer. Now he was here to offer encouragment at group level. With him would sometimes appear another frequent visitor to airbases, Capt. Eddie Rickenbacker, a hero of even longer standing and the virtual personification of air combat's birth.

But when Rickenbacker comes to address Frederic Arnold's P-38 squadron, the author of *Doorknob Five Two* is forced to admit that the old man seems a bit irrelevant. For one thing, his voice barely carries past the second row, where the fighter pilots—chugging a special shipment of beer in celebration of their unit's recent successes—find it hard to concentrate on anything but the brew. Yet Arnold does listen, only to regretfully discount what the famous man has to say, rambling on as he does about shooting down "Huns" for an America that "wanted aces":

> I knew he was trying to inspire us, to raise our morale, but he was simply a stranger from a different time and place, a time that knew nothing about modern specialized flying technique, about tight formation, disciplined bomber escort, dive bombing, squadron concentration for effective fire power. On the ground, I didn't know the names of replacement pilots, but in the air, their planes meshed within the rigid framework of the squadron. There were no heroic aces chasing after enemy fighters on their own. The squadron was the strength. Each plane was part of the whole, connected to the same machine. If a piece was defective, it was replaced (1984, p. 223).

Perhaps, in the flashier ETO, pilots like John Godfrey and Chuck Yeager were listening to Captain Eddie and taking it more to heart. Flying from England and tangling with the yellow-nosed "Abbeville Boys" of the Luftwaffe's crack fighter units may well have seemed a bit like the last war, while in the MTO it seemed more like the next. Certainly, the air war from England fit the requirements for journalistic glamorization, and maybe its closer affinities with public conceptions made the mythmaking easier. And, with the myth established, at least part of reality could conform.

There was no such thing in the Mediterranean. In this theater, which had opened up in Casablanca where in the popular imagination Humphrey Bogart looked into Ingrid Bergman's eyes while the pianist played and sang "As Time Goes By," flyers made up different words to go with the familiar melody, a just-as-convincing song that ended like this:

> It's still the same old story
> The Eighth gets all the glory
> While we're the ones who die.
> The odds are always too damned high
> As flak goes by.

Conclusion

Victims

A SIGNAL CONTRIBUTION of strategic air warfare is that it can be fought without directly facing the enemy. There are victims of such strategy, of course, but they are not engaged in their personhood. No fighter ace ever listed his bag of kills as so many German pilots; rather, his victories were over Messerschmitts and Focke-Wulfs. Likewise, no bomber mission was ever described as against "the people of Berlin"; instead, the target was named "Berlin" itself, as if tons of explosives were being dropped on an abstraction. From 20,000 feet, often through solid undercast and with guidance only by a scarcely understood new device called radar, whatever lay down below surely seemed abstract to the men who flew these missions. And among the fighter escort, pilots like Hub Zemke, Frances Gabreski, John Godfrey, and Chuck Yeager were measuring themselves not against another pilot's strength but rather by what their planes could do. Infantry soldiers fought not the bayonet but the Wehrmacht trooper who wielded it; P-51 pilots were thinking not of how strong or tall their Luftwaffe adversary might be, but whether he was in a tight-turning Me-109 or a fast-diving, heavily armored FW-190. A "kill" meant the plane went down, not that its pilot died. Indeed, many memoirists are happy when the pilot survives, and some take care to see that this happens, as if bailing out completes the terms of combat.

American flyers' own losses are, with notable exceptions, almost equally abstract. Among the fighter pilots flying from England a tradition developed that lost colleagues were not talked about; in some squadrons this went so far as not even mentioning the victim's name, as if he had never existed. Such focusing is another limit to the terms of combat: no past (distinguished by its losses) and no future either (given statistical chances stacked against any one man's survival), just an intense concentration on the present where they all lived. This attitude helps make possible the remarkable post-war friendships between former adversaries, celebrated meetings of pilots who have last seen each other through the gunsights of a Mustang and a Messerschmitt.

Because their own combat experience may have included the important exception to such abstraction—having a wounded man on board—bomber crews seem less given to this after-the-battle camaraderie with former enemies than do the fighter pilots. Struggling to save the life of a waist gunner torn up by explosive shells from an attacking Focke-Wulf makes crewmen less eager to spend later years over brandy and cigars with German flyers. The possibility of such encounters is rare, in any case, because were a bomber to suffer so severe an attack, chances are that it never made it back to base. Here the lost plane creates an even greater vacancy, a loss ten times as bad: four empty beds in officers' quarters, six empty cots where the enlisted men bunk. Ten times as much, in other words, to not talk about, ten more reasons to see this side of the air war abstractly.

Not that vacancy and abstraction don't occupy their own spaces. They do, and every bomber crew memoir gives them plenty of thought. Inevitably, if the author was a bombardier, these thoughts become deep introspection. Fred Koger performed that job on B-17s over Germany, and in *Countdown!* reflects on how these matters crept up on him during his tour. On leave in London he witnesses a V-1 attack and is impressed by how shaken is the WAAF he's dating; the flying bomb has landed far from them, but she still tenses from memories of the Blitz, when danger was closer and more frequent.

"I began to realize what a different perspective I had about the war," Koger realizes here. "I really hadn't talked seriously to anyone who had been in the heart of the battle from the start and had a burning hatred, a desire for revenge." This is, in fact, another abstraction: the American bomber offensive from England did not get underway until long after the Luftwaffe's assault on London, Coventry, and other cities had come to an end. Now young men like himself find it hard to see themselves as striking back with any personal motivation. "I didn't hate the Germans," Koger recalls:

They were just the enemy and when I toggled out a load of bombs it was with no more emotion than trying to powder a clay target on the skeet range. The target was only a far-away pattern of buildings and roads and checkpoints five miles below. And when I leaned forward to watch the bomb strike it was to see if the bursts were in the right part of that pattern. I never had any mental picture of bodies flying through the air, or people scream-ing, or houses burning (1990, p. 137).

In *Target Ploesti: View from a Bombsight* Leroy Newby has simi-lar thoughts, as do most of his fellow bombardiers. It's the advice of their chaplain, Newby explains, that "helped us keep our sanity." How to do that was simple: treat the business abstractly. "The smart-est thing we could do as individuals," Newby and his buddies are told, "was to put what happened on the ground below out of our minds. Keep it impersonal." Their targets are military; as for military issues, remember that "We didn't start the war." In the long run, more lives would be saved by acting now. Besides, "If any of us would falter and let it get us down, there would be someone to take our place the next day" (1983, p. 98). With this mix of abstraction and pragmatism, Newby fights on. Yet at times readers find him doing a very unchaplain-like thing (at least for the religious counseling in his outfit), saying a prayer for the civilians below each time he sights a load of bombs on Ploesti.

No American bomber force was ever turned back by enemy op-position. Neither was any such attack repelled by force of con-science. The closest that may have come to happening were two specific raids, one on Münster from England late in 1943, the other against Munich from Italy in 1944. The big exception in planning these raids is that there are no strategic targets—just the cities themselves, with the goal of demoralizing the citizenry. The Münster raid is especially worrying to the men of the Ninth Bomb Group quoted in Ian Hawkins's *B-17s Over Berlin*. Given these details, the group's lead navigator, Capt. Ellis B. Scripture, is "shocked to learn that we were to bomb civilians as our primary target for the first time in the war and that our aiming point was to be the front steps of the Münster Cathedral at noon on Sunday, just as mass was completed" (1990, p. 66). Scripture is very reluctant to fly this mis-sion, and does so only against the threat of being court martialed, just a bit mollified that the bombing time has been moved to three o'clock.

Going for Munich with the idea of setting it ablaze is equally ab-horrent to William R. Cubbins, a pilot with the Fifteenth Air Force.

He knows that both bomber air forces, the Eighth and the Fifteenth, have prided themselves on following the unique American practice of pinpoint aiming. The RAF and USAAF had debated the issue, almost to the point of having the Americans' daylight precision policy changed to follow the RAF's night bombing program; only Churchill's fancy for the phrase "around the clock bombing" saved the U.S. initiative. But now, Cubbins laments, "We were going to follow England's lead in the war and 'terror bomb.' That was the 'new bad,' and I didn't like it." His reasons sum up much of what has kept bomber crews at their jobs and signal a turning point in his *The War of the Cottontails* (1989):

> Heretofore I'd never thought of our raids as being against people. We bombed targets. I'd never liked the obvious side effect, but neither had I tried to fool myself. I'd accepted the certainty that civilians would be killed by our raids against military targets. But to bomb them intentionally—the idea was reprehensible. That was the sort of thing the Nazis did in Holland, at Coventry: the list is long. But this wasn't a game we were playing. We could well die on this, or the next, mission. With that rationale reinforcing my will, I directed my thinking to mission details (p. 69).

And so Cubbins soldiers on, his professionalism and dependence on his own skills more important than the issues whose morality lies on the conscience of planners. As for the doers, most of them are probably like Bert Stiles, who flies mission after mission without enthusiasm. "Day after day we were on the list, for a trip to Berlin or Nancy or Munich or somewhere," he writes (as if with a sigh) in *Serenade to the Big Bird.* "We weren't meeting any new people, or learning anything constructive, or deepening our understanding or cementing any friendships." What he and his crewmates do is simple: "We just went up there and over, to knock the hell out of some city with the vague hope that some day that city will be rebuilt for some people we can get along with." Not a very good way of doing things, he realizes— "and when the day turns up that we can start using other methods, I'm going to be one of the gladder people in the world" (1947, p. 70).

Where American flyers do meet potential victims is in the air. Here, quite apart from the abstraction of facing death, is an immediate present that can be dealt with. Precisely because most encounters are between machine and machine, human recognition is a rare and therefore special occurrence. As such, it is often one that is treasured, thanks to the way such meetings encapsulate the key elements of air combat.

It takes courage and skills to fly in such circumstances, and most memoirists have abundant praise for these aspects of their enemies. As a group commander, Dale Smith does his flying at the head of a massive B-17 formation, and from here he can witness the head-on attacks mounted by Luftwaffe fighters in the face of concentrated firepower. "I could actually see the cone of fire with the enemy at its apex," he recalls in *Screaming Eagle*, "and I marveled at the courage of those German pilots, who could drive home their attacks against such a hail of death" (1990, p. 47). All the more remarkable, therefore, when Elmer Bendiner sees a Me-109 come through the formation this way without his guns firing. This is certainly not the intention, but a temperature inversion has sealed his guns, just as the B-17's armament has been frozen over. Here, in this "moment when a meteorological happenstance imposed a truce," as Bendiner phrases it in *The Fall of Fortresses*, the enemies cannot hurl death at one another. So what do they do? They wave, close enough for the Americans to see that their adversary has a black mustache (1980, p. 246). One of Donald Currier's sharpest memories in *50 Mission Crush* is of a lone Messerschmitt blazing through a full squadron of B-24s. "There is courage enough to go around for everyone, friend and foe alike, who flies and fights in the wild blue yonder," Currier reflects (1993, p. 122).

When the same thing happens to John Comer's formation in *Combat Crew*, their appreciation of the lone pilot's courage goes a bit farther. Here the Me-109 has approached from the rear, swung ahead in a wide circle, and takes on the B-17s by himself. "Look at that bastard," Comer's navigator calls to the crew, "—did you ever see such guts?" Their reaction is remarkable but not atypical of emotions one encounters in such memoirs:

> What did a military formation do to a gallant airman blithely taking on deadly odds? The book said shoot him down, but that went against the grain of American admiration for courage beyond the ordinary. And in a hopeless cause. We easily could— and perhaps from a military point of view should—have destroyed that fighter. But there was some chivalry left in the American makeup. Without a word of consultation with each other, all of our gunners came up with the same decision: they held their fire. The formation opened up to let him blaze through. How could we kill a man with such foolhardy courage? It is seldom that men see an example of pure nobility. That German expected to die on his assault. It was foolish of course but, like the British cavalry's "Charge of the Light Brigade," it was a thrilling spectacle to watch (1988, p. 249).

That individuals on both sides are capable of such acts—both of shooting and not shooting, as happens in Comer's example—allows a momentary but very welcome glimpse of the human dimension in this abstract and heavily mechanical style of warfare. In *Target Ploesti* bombardier Leroy Newby, busy with his calculations, can only hear descriptions of a head-on attack taking place. Soon he notices something else, the attacker's bullets ripping through his B-24. But the high point comes when he glances out to see "the invaders sweeping past at lightning speed, swastikas glistening in the sun, and one pilot's arm poised in salute. Just like in the movies. He was to be the only enemy soldier I would see in the war" (1983, p. 31). But as in Comer's passage, seeing a Messerschmitt or Focke-Wulf doing something that takes extraordinary pilot courage lets a human face show through as well. Courage, or in some instances vulnerability—both are human attributes, and prompt appropriate responses, such as from Capt. Ellis Scripture, navigating a gigantic formation of fifteen bombardment groups to Münster. Up ahead of the bomber stream is a single Me-410 who in turning away from a previous attack is flying slowly. No one wants to fire at him, but they must, for he is quite literally blocking their path. "As one who had grown up on stories of fair fights in Western novels and stories of First World War dog fights," Scripture is quoted in *B-17s Over Berlin*, "I could take no particular pleasure in shooting down a guy who was trying to run away, even though he came in shooting and had undoubtedly been firing at other B-17s in our formation just previously" (1990, p. 71).

There is at least one other time when American gunners do not fire, but ironically so that a German fighter can. The occasion, described by Leroy Newby in *Target Ploesti*, is when in the process of bailing out one crew member from a flaming B-17 suffers the nightmare of having his parachute caught on the bomb-bay door. Here he dangles, being pulled beneath the stricken and abandoned plane to a slow and surely hideous death.

"Then the war kind of hesitated," as Newby reports, "when a German ME-109 flew right into the belly of the enemy—the middle of the formation of bombers." Scores if not hundreds of gunners look on, "amazed that he had the guts to fly into the center of all those guns pointing at him. The war halted as everyone quit shooting. The German gently eased up to the helpless airman and shot him. Not another shot was fired as he peeled off and went on his way. They let him go, and the war started again" (1983, p. 131).

More prevalent are the other parachute stories where Luftwaffe fighter pilots don't fire. The whole notion of killing an aviator while in such descent is a controversial and even notorious one, but the issue is clear in international law. Persons bailing out over their own territory are considered still in combat, given that they can be expected to resume fighting after they land. Over enemy territory, however, the parachuting flyer is *hors de combat* once he abandons his plane, for it is prisoner-of-war status that awaits him on the ground. From the Allied point of view, however, the propaganda works all against the Germans. Over England in the Battle of Britain, they have the legal right and tactical imperative to shoot at RAF pilots in parachutes; yet doing so costs them immensely in moral suasion. Now, three and four years later in the great air battles over their own land, where skies are sometimes filled with the billowing silk canopies of descending Americans, the rules say they cannot shoot. Obviously, many do. But as the years lengthen and wartime animosities are put to rest, stories of Luftwaffe planes withholding their fire become more numerous. As they do, memoirists strive to interpret these actions not as legalities but as further evidence that the real war is something abstract, between machine and machine. Such is how Keith Schuyler puts it in *Elusive Horizons* when his own crew bails out and one of them is approached by the victorious fighter: "The 190 did come in on Schow. Hanging helpless, Schow just waved. The German waved back. He had his kill—chalk up one more B-24" (1992, p. 147).

On the U.S. side, fighter pilots pride themselves on their professionalism. That professionalism makes them interested in how their adversaries do their jobs, and once thinking begins along those lines it is not long before the individual is being considered. In *Mustang Ace*, Robert Goebel has the chance to inspect a captured Messerschmitt:

> I threw a leg over the cockpit edge, climbed in, and sat down. I grasped the stick, put my left hand on the throttle, slid my feet forward into the rudder pedals, and sat transfixed.
>
> Who had sat like this before me? Did he squeeze this trigger and shoot these guns? Had he shot down a Hurricane or a Beaufighter? I had no love for the Luftwaffe, but I was flying with that German pilot in the skies over Europe—touching the things he touched, looking through the same sight he once looked through (1991, p. 69).

This style of identification makes it easier for Goebel to show mercy when shooting down an active Me-109, circling the descending pilot carefully (so as not to collapse his parachute) and giving the customary salute. This sympathy extends to a later engagement when an enemy's cockpit canopy whips off before Goebel can stop firing. "I had never seen the actual death of one of my adversaries before," he laments; "it was unnerving. It had not been deliberate, but I must have hit him as he came out, and I wondered if I could have been a split second faster in releasing the trigger. But there was no time to worry about that now, unless I wanted to join him" (p. 188).

Then there are the face-to-face meetings. In accounts written during the war, the slant is one that favors power over the enemy, such as the story told by Maj. Richard Thruelsen and Lt. Elliott Arnold in *Mediterranean Sweep* (1944) of how a P-39 Airacobra pilot not only shot down a Me-109 in the desert but hurried back to base, borrowed a jeep, and rode out to capture his victim personally; only after this do the narrators confide that the victorious American also took his opposite number to the hospital where this Condor Legion veteran of the Spanish Civil War recovers (p. 80). It is afterwards, in a memoir dedicated to issues of sensitivity and the contrary forces of human kindness and cruelty, that the remarkable (and almost unbelievable) incidents are recounted.

Topping the bill is Frederic Arnold's tale in *Doorknob Five Two* of his encounters with a Luftwaffe fighter pilot. Shot down over Italy during a low-level P-38 raid, Arnold is met by a Messerschmitt pilot full of questions. The highlight of their conversation is the German's query about something he's witnessed earlier on when Arnold had circled an airman in a dinghy, watching out for him until help arrived.

"Would you have saved him if you knew he was German?"

"Sure, why not?" Arnold answers. As if in recompense, the Luftwaffe pilot identifies himself as the one who shot him down, prompting Arnold to note that this adversary could easily have finished him off, but didn't.

Why not? "This is not important" (1984, p. 12), he's told, but as the memoir continues—including Arnold's escape and return to flying—it's obvious that such issues will arise again.

It happens when Arnold's squadron intercepts three lumbering German transport planes. Ready to shoot them down, the P-38 pilots suddenly hear a German voice urging them to relent, that the aircraft are carrying American prisoners. Recognizing the voice of his old enemy, Arnold is prone to let them pass, only to watch in horror as his nemesis in the squadron shoots them down, U.S. casualties or not.

In the process, the Luftwaffe pilot exhausts his reserves of fuel. Learning this, Arnold directs him to a nearby American base on Sicily where he calls ahead to clear the Messerschmitt for landing. All is made secure for this most considerate of German flyers when something goes wrong: as the plane comes in to land, members of a tank crew not in touch with airfield communications blow it out of the sky, perhaps thinking that they're protecting the unwary P-38 nearby.

Structured like a perfect work of fiction and encompassing all the large and small issues of Arnold's experience in the war, this narrative tests a reader's credibility. Yet in the context of so many other adversary stories, it seems a next logical step. In disclaimers to his book Frederic Arnold is sufficiently worried about damaging truths to have changed the name of his squadron tormentor under threat of legal action. Had *Doorknob Five Two* been fiction and presented as such, there would be no such risks. That Arnold takes them implies that the story is a true one, for his nemesis's offense in shooting down the American prisoners is his only seriously culpable act, the rest of his behavior being simple, if vile, anti-Semitism.

If there's a moral here, it is the one Eugene Fletcher learns during the training segment of *The Lucky Bastard Club*. From the safety of California this future B-17 pilot has few worries about the Luftwaffe. Instead, he's being menaced by an egregiously unfair instructor who has butted into a situation of which he's ignorant. Reporting the incident to his own instructor, the author must have shown his hurt and confusion, for these are the consolations that are supplied: "Fletch, there is one thing you cadets have to realize and that is you're probably being trained to shoot down, in some instances, better people than you are being trained to protect" (1993, p. 156).

There is one place where the air war fully ceases being abstract and mechanical, and that's when flyers find themselves on the ground. To some extent it can happen from England, such as when bomber crews on leave in London see remnants of destruction from the Blitz three years before and wonder what Germany must look like now that it's receiving thousands of times the tonnage. Near the end of William A. Ong's *Target Luftwaffe* (1981) Col. Ken Martin reports his amazement when being bombed in Nuremberg as a freshly captured prisoner of war. From a trench he can see the lead ships coming with their marking flares, followed by consecutive waves with their explosives. "Roaring fires broke out," he notes, "infiltrated with black smoke. The flames climbed high in the sky, so that the low moon appeared blood-red. I watched several bombers, hit by artillery fire, fall like flaming meteors" (p. 289). As an airman, his attention is first given to the skies. But soon what's happening on the ground consumes his interest: "I've read many colorful accounts of bombing by writers handy with words. But I don't think you adequately can describe, in conversation or in writing, the terror of a bombing raid; the fire and the smoke and the burning, falling planes, all enveloped in an inferno of noise. I've thought about it a great deal, but I still don't understand how the German people took it as long as they did" (p. 290).

In the war of attrition destined by the Allies' policy of unconditional surrender to be fought until Berlin itself was occupied, the Germans did take it. This policy was the result of no small abstraction; because despite their success at working together, the Allied governments did not trust one another sufficiently to allow a negotiated peace. The greatest fears were on Russia's part, fueled by Stalin's own paranoia of Western intentions. But having Russia in the war confused the Anglo-American alliance, because the third party involved was a politically hot one whose intentions were not known. These same Allies had determined, at the Casablanca Conference early in 1943, that strategic bombing would be the Allies' primary weapon. Not just tactical targets but the enemy's war-making ability would be destroyed. And that meant bomb after bomb after bomb, right to the bitter end.

For one American flyer, operating with the Ninety-fifth Bomb Group from England, that war came to an end on a mission over Augsburg on 16 March 1944. Navigator Charles Brennan describes his capture and subsequent interrogation for Ian Hawkins in *B-17s Over Berlin*.

He has much to be thankful for. His crew has all bailed out safely, their pilot being last to leave, just before the plane explodes. All land safely. All are captured without incident, no small feat at a time when angry civilians might dispatch such "terror flyers" with pitchforks, shotguns, or a hangman's rope; more than one American was thrown into the flames of his crashed bomber. Brennan and his buddies eventually arrive at their permanent camp, Stalag Luft III, Sagan, the day after the "great escape" of subsequent book and movie fame. Here, too, a bullet of sorts is dodged, for had Brennan's men taken part in the breakout they could have been among those captured and shot.

In ending their war, all seems to be going well for the crew of this B-17. But as they are being transported from interrogation to encampment something intervenes, something that proves their greatest danger so far: the continuing air war itself. The occasion is a raid on Frankfurt, where the POWs are being held in train cars on a siding east of the city. Here they survive, but their interrogation center is flattened behind them.

Yet there is one more problem. Throughout this ordeal, the Americans have been without food and water. With Allied bombers up above threatening their lives as indiscriminately as those of the Germans, Brennan and his crew find themselves in the straits usually imposed on their enemies; in an otherwise abstract air war, they are now on the receiving end. And what do they receive? Not an Allied bomb on their rail car, and not an attack by enraged German civilians. Instead, they are noticed by passengers aboard another train that has been shunted to this siding: a company of Wehrmacht infantrymen en route to the Eastern Front.

What transpires is more remarkable than Lieutenant Brennan reports it, for his mention is of just one more incident on the way to Sagan and his year as a prisoner of war. "Some of the soldiers," he mentions, "when they realized who we were, came over to our train and gave us some of their water and rations" (1990, p. 223). Here, beyond all mechanisms and abstractions, is an intimation not of how wars are fought but how they can end.

Bibliography

Alexander, Richard L. *They Called Me Dixie.* Hemet, Calif.: Robinson Typographics, 1988.

Anderson, Clarence E. "Bud." *To Fly and Fight.* New York: St. Martin's Press, 1990.

Anderson, William. *Pathfinders.* London: Jarrolds, 1946.

Ardery, Philip. *Bomber Pilot.* Lexington, Ky.: University Press of Kentucky, 1978.

Arnold, Frederic. *Doorknob Five Two.* Los Angeles: S.E. Maxwell, 1984.

Arnold, H.H. *Global Mission.* New York: Harper & Brothers, 1949.

Beck, L.C., Jr. *Fighter Pilot.* Huntington Park, Calif.: Mr. and Mrs. L.C. Beck, 1946.

Bendiner, Elmer. *The Fall of Fortresses.* New York: Putnam's, 1980.

Bledsoe, Marvin. *Thunderbolt.* New York: Van Nostrand Reinhold, 1982.

Brickhill, Paul. *The Dam Busters.* London: Evans, 1951.

———. *Reach for the Sky: The Story of Douglas Bader.* London: Collins, 1954.

Bridgeman, William (with Jacqueline Hazard). *The Lonely Sky.* New York: Henry Holt, 1955.

Byers, Richard G. *Attack.* Fayetteville, Ark.: Aardvark Books, 1984.

Caine, Philip D. *Eagles of the RAF: The World War II Eagle Squadrons.* Washington, D.C.: National Defense University Press, 1991.

Carson, Leonard. *Pursue and Destroy.* Granada Hills, Calif.: Sentry, 1978.

Charlwood, Don. *Journeys into Night.* Hawthorn, Victoria, Australia: Hudson, 1991.

Childers, James Saxon. *War Eagles.* New York: Appleton-Century, 1943.

Colgan, Bill. *World War II Fighter-Bomber Pilot.* Manhattan, Kans.: Sunflower University Press, 1988.

Comer, John. *Combat Crew.* New York: William Morrow, 1988.

Crosby, Harry H. *A Wing and a Prayer.* New York: HarperCollins, 1993.

Cubbins, William R. *The War of the Cottontails.* Chapel Hill, N. Car.: Algonquin, 1989.

Currier, Donald R. *50 Mission Crush.* Shippensburg, Penn.: Burd Street Press, 1992. (Reprint. New York: Pocket Books, 1993.)

Davis, Benjamin O., Jr. *Benjamin O. Davis, Jr.: An Autobiography.* Washington, D.C.: Smithsonian Institution Press, 1991.

Donahue, Arthur Gerald. *Last Flight from Singapore.* New York: Macmillan, 1943.

———. *Tally Ho! Yankee in a Spitfire.* New York: Macmillan, 1943.

Douglas, W. Sholto. Combat and Command. New York: Simon & Schuster, 1966.

Dunn, William R. *Fighter Pilot.* Lexington, Ky.: University Press of Kentucky, 1982.

Ethell, Jeffrey L., and Alfred Price. *Target Berlin / Mission 250: 6 March 1944.* London: Arms and Armour, 1989.

Fagan, Vincent F. *Liberator Pilot: The Cottontails' Battle for Oil.* Carlsbad, Calif.: California Aero Press, 1991.

Fletcher, Eugene. *Fletcher's Gang.* Seattle, Wash.: University of Washington Press, 1988.

———. *Mister.* Seattle, Wash.: University of Washington Press, 1991. In *The Lucky Bastard Club.* Seattle, Wash.: University of Washington Press, 1993.

Freeman, Roger A. *Zemke's Wolf Pack.* New York: Crown, 1988. (Reprint. New York: Pocket Books, 1991.)

Friedheim, Eric, and Samuel W. Taylor. *Fighters Up.* London: Nicholson & Watson, 1944.

Gabreski, Francis. *Gabby: A Fighter Pilot's Life.* New York: Orion, 1991.

Genovese, J. Gen. *We Flew Without Guns.* Philadelphia: Winston, 1945.

Gibson, Guy. *Enemy Coast Ahead.* London: Michael Joseph, 1946.

Godfrey, John T. *The Look of Eagles.* New York: Random House, 1958.

Goebel, Robert J. *Mustang Ace.* Pacifica, Calif.: Pacifica Press, 1991.

Goodson, James A. *Tumult in the Clouds.* New York: St. Martin's Press, 1983.

Haugland, Vern. *The Eagle Squadrons: Yanks in the RAF, 1940-1942.* New York: Ziff-Davis, 1979.

————. *The Eagles' War: The Saga of the Eagle Squadron Pilots, 1940-1945*. New York: Aronson, 1982. (Reprint Blue Ridge Summit, Pa.: TAB Aero, 1992.)

Hawkins, Ian L., ed. *B-17s Over Berlin*. Washington, D.C.: Brassey's US, 1990.

Heller, Joseph. *Catch-22*. New York: Simon and Schuster, 1961.

Hillary, Richard. *The Last Enemy*. London: Macmillan, 1942.

Howard, James H. *Roar of the Tiger*. New York: Orion, 1991.

Hutton, Bud, and Andy Rooney. *Air Gunner*. New York: Farrar & Rinehart, 1944.

Ilfrey, Jack. *Happy Jack's Go-Buggy*. Smithtown, N.Y.: Exposition Press, 1979.

Jakeman, Robert J. *The Divided Skies: Established Segregated Flight Training at Tuskegee, Alabama, 1924-1942*. Tuscaloosa, Ala.: University of Alabama Press, 1992.

Johnson, Johnnie. *Wing Leader*. London: Chatto & Windus, 1956.

Johnson, Robert S. *Thunderbolt!* New York: Ballantine, 1959. (Reprint. New York: Bantam, 1990, with Martin Caidin.)

Kenneily, Byron. *The Eagles Roar!* New York: Harper & Brothers, 1942.

Klinkowitz, Jerome. *Their Finest Hours: Narratives of the RAF and Luftwaffe in World War II*. Ames, Iowa: Iowa State University Press, 1989.

Koger, Fred. *Countdown!* Chapel Hill, N. Car.: Algonquin, 1990.

Lane, Brian [as "B.J. Ellan"]. *Spitfire!* London: John Murray, 1942.

Lay, Beirne, Jr. *I've Had It: The Survival of a Bomb Group Commander*. New York: Harper & Brothers, 1945.

Lundgren, William R. *Across the High Frontier*. New York: Morrow, 1955.

McClendon, Dennis E. *The Lady Be Good: Mystery Bomber of World War II*. Blue Ridge Summit, Penn.: TAB Aero, 1982.

McFarland, Stephen L., and Wesley Phillips Newton. *To Command the Skies: The Battle for Air Superiority Over Germany, 1942-1944*. Washington, D.C.: Smithsonian Institution Press, 1991.

McGuire, Melvin W. *Bloody Skies*. Las Cruces, N. Mex.: Yucca Tree Press, 1993.

Matt, John. *Crewdog*. Hamilton, Va.: Waterford, 1992.

Morrison, Wilbur H. *Fortress Without a Roof: The Allied Bombing of the Third Reich*. New York: St. Martin's, 1982.

Muirhead, John. *Those Who Fall*. New York: Random House, 1986.

Newby, Leroy W. *Into the Guns of Ploesti*. Osceola, Wisc.: Motorbooks International, 1991.

————. *Target Ploesti: View from a Bombsight*. Novato, Calif.: Presidio Press, 1983.

Noah, Joe, and Samuel L. Sox, Jr. *George Preddy, Top Mustang Ace.* Osceola, Wisc.: Motorbooks International, 1991.

Olmsted, Merle. *The 357th Over Europe.* St. Paul, Minn.: Phalanx, 1994.

O'Neil, Brian D. *Half a Wing, Three Engines, and a Prayer: B-17s Over Germany.* Blue Ridge Summit, Penn.: TAB Aero, 1989.

Ong, William A. *Target Luftwaffe.* Kansas City, Mo.: Lowell Press, 1981.

Perret, Geoffrey. *Winged Victory: The Army Air Forces in World War II.* New York: Random House, 1993.

Price, Bill. *Close Calls.* Usk, Wash.: Aviation Usk, 1992.

Redding, John M., and Harold Leyshon. *Skyways to Berlin.* Indianapolis, Ind.: Bobbs-Merrill, 1943.

Richey, Paul. *Fighter Pilot.* London: B.T. Batsford, 1941.

Sandler, Stanley. *Segregated Skies: All-Black Combat Squadrons of World War II.* Washington, D.C.: Smithsonian Institution Press, 1992.

Savage, Mark. *Those Were the Days.* Dublin, Ohio: Markas Publishing, 1993.

Schaffer, Ronald. *Wings of Judgment: American Bombing in World War II.* New York: Oxford University Press, 1985.

Schuyler, Keith C. *Elusive Horizons.* S. Brunswick, N.J.: A.S. Barnes, 1969. (Reprint. New York: Avon, 1992).

Smallwood, J.W. *Tomlin's Crew.* Manhattan, Kans.: Sunflower University Press, 1992.

Smith, Ben, Jr. *Chick's Crew.* Tallahassee, Fla.: Rose Printing, 1978.

Smith, Dale O., III. *Screaming Eagle.* Chapel Hill, N.Car.: Algonquin, 1990.

Steinbeck, John. *Bombs Away: The Story of a Bomber Team.* New York: Viking, 1942.

Stiles, Bert. *Serenade to the Big Bird.* New York: W.W. Norton, 1947. (Reprint. London: Lindsay Drummond, 1947.)

Thruelsen, Richard, and Elliott Arnold. *Mediterranean Sweep.* New York: Duell, Sloan & Pearce, 1944.

Turner, Richard E. *Big Friend, Little Friend.* Garden City, N.Y.: Doubleday, 1969.

Wolfe, Tom. *The Right Stuff.* New York: Farrar, Straus & Giroux, 1979.

Wordell, M.T., and E.N. Seiler. *"Wildcats" Over Casablanca.* Boston: Little, Brown, 1943.

Yeager, Chuck (with Leo Janos). *Yeager.* New York: Bantam, 1985.

Index